# GROWING IN FAITH

## The Lee Abbey Story

### Richard More

**HODDER AND STOUGHTON**
LONDON  SYDNEY  AUCKLAND  TORONTO

**British Library Cataloguing in Publication Data**

More, Richard
  Growing in Faith
  1. Christian communities – England – Lynton (Devon)
  2. Lee Abbey – History
  I. Title
  267'.09423'52      BV4406.G/

ISBN 0 340 26353 9

# Foreword

I welcome and am happy to commend this new Lee Abbey story, bringing the previous Lee Abbey story up to date and supplementing it with many details with which I was certainly not familiar before. My wife and I owe an incalculable debt to Lee Abbey, dating from the time when we went there with our family in 1952. We were frequent visitors after that and we have watched it 'growing in faith' all the time. In the course of its history it has contributed to the Church of England lay ministers annointed with the Spirit and willing to witness to Christ, and clergy revitalised and given new hope. It has provided an example of community life which has been copied elsewhere. And not least it has given tens of thousands of people holidays which they will always remember, holidays with a difference, holidays with a purpose, holidays with a blessing.

Those of you who already know Lee Abbey will find in this book many aspects of its life you can identify with, and those of you who have not visited it might well be inspired to do so to discover for yourselves new sources of spiritual life and a new understanding of the Gospel.

Stuart Ebor:
Bishopthorpe, York
1st March 1982

# Contents

# Introduction

It often happens that the person who makes the suggestion gets landed with the job! So it has been with this book.

Before I became a member of the Community four years ago, Lee Abbey was little more than a name to me. It appeared to be one of those enigmatic Christian centres that did not quite fit in with the normal Church structures.

Sharing in the Community's life and ministry, I have become increasingly conscious that the development of Lee Abbey must be counted as one of the notable works of the Holy Spirit in recent years. So came my suggestion that there should be a new book, that both those familiar and those unfamiliar with Lee Abbey should know something of the daring faith upon which it was founded and has grown, and its witness to the faithfulness and power of God at work.

When Jack Winslow wrote *The Lee Abbey Story* twenty-five years ago, he could draw upon his own experience. My information has had to be culled from many sources and I am most grateful to the many people who have known Lee Abbey over the years and have answered my questions. I have endeavoured to bring the story up to date and, in a way that was not possible then, put the first years in a more historical setting. The facts, I hope, are accurate; the opinions and reflections are of course purely my own. I am also very grateful to the present Community at Lee Abbey for all their help, patience and encouragement, and especially to Catherine Alexander for her hours of work in typing and retyping the manuscript, to Anna Cameron and Gay Perry for many helpful suggestions, to Gill Titmuss for the drawing of the estate, and to Phyllis Sutton for many of the photographs.

In the introduction to his book Jack wrote, 'We could easily give the appearance of presumption, and of a desire to glorify Lee Abbey rather than to advance the Kingdom of God. If at any point we are near to be doing this we would ask the reader to forgive us . . .'

I humbly make the same request.

Lee Abbey,
Ascension Day, 1981

## Prologue

The famous Valley of Rocks, situated on the very edge of Exmoor near the village of Lynton, presents a spectacular sight. On the one side is the steep hillside littered with small boulders and covered with gorse and bracken, while on the other rise great mounds of rock which drop away into the sea, thus creating in one place one of the highest sea cliffs in England. The weird shapes created by the rocks and the bleakness of the landscape have caused it to be compared to the surface of the moon. Even today it is not hard to imagine the legendary John Ridd riding through this valley to consult Mother Meldrum about his beloved Lorna Doone.

Among the visitors to the Valley of Rocks one afternoon in June 1932 was a young curate from Cheltenham, spending a few days holidaying with his sister. It was their first visit, and after looking at the Valley of Rocks itself, they decided to follow the road to see where it led. As they walked uphill, it looked as if the road was going to come to a dead end, but suddenly rounding a bend they found that they were walking down through another wider and very different valley. There were fields on either side; the hillside was wooded; and there was a small golf course. Passing an imposing, ivy-clad stone tower, they continued down the road and a most magnificent view came into sight. The valley, bordered by steep woodlands on either side, sloped down to a small sunlit bay. Beyond that could be seen another bay, and beyond that yet another series of cliffs rising majestically out of the sea. As the previous valley had been austere and barren, so this one was welcoming and lush. The scene was breathtaking in its beauty.

Turning to look at the building which enjoyed this exquisite view, they saw a large Victorian mansion, much of its exterior hidden by creepers, nestling in the slope of the hillside. Wondering what such a magnificent building could be, they retraced their steps back to the tower, to find that a notice-board provided the answer. THE LEE ABBEY HOTEL, *An Historic House remodelled and brought up to date*. They looked wistfully at the tariff. 'One thing is certain, you and I will never stay there,' said the young man. And they continued their walk down to the bay.

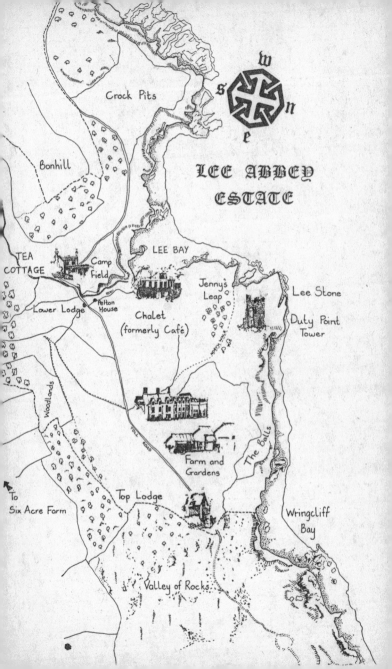

# GROWING IN FAITH

# 1

## Beginnings

At the time of his holiday in 1932, Roger de Pemberton was a curate in Cheltenham. It was to be another ten years before he visited Lee Abbey again, but God was already laying the foundation for the part that he was to play with others in establishing a ministry based on that remote West-Country hotel.

Roger was a Christian with a strong evangelical background, and a deep desire to bring people to personal faith in Jesus Christ. Like many of his contemporaries, he had become involved in leading campaigns run by The Children's Special Service Mission (C.S.S.M.) in the late 1920s. During his time at Cambridge, first as an undergraduate at St. Catherine's College and then as an ordinand at Ridley Hall, three successive Easters found him running a mission at Cheltenham directed mainly at the Boys' and Ladies' Colleges. 1929, however, saw the last of these campaigns as the leaders felt that they were getting into a rut. Yet with over a hundred contacts they were reluctant to allow these to lapse, so they were looking for some way of following them up with regular Christian teaching.

It was then that the idea of a magazine was mooted, and although Roger had had no experience of publishing, he had no shortage of enthusiasm. Approaching the Headquarters of the C.S.S.M. he persuasively presented his idea but they were unwilling to provide any financial backing. This was not sufficient to deter Roger, who was by now very keen on the idea; he decided that if the C.S.S.M. would not help him, he would produce it himself. This was the same determination that was later to be needed, when the time came for founding Lee Abbey. A vast number of letters were sent out to possible readers and before the first copy was produced in 1930, around 3,000 subscribers had been procured. The magazine was called *The Pathfinder*, and proved very popular; the circulation quickly rose to 6,000 within three years. Soon the whole project had to be put on a more organised business footing than was possible at the beginning, when it was edited in his bedroom at his parents' home in Worthing. Now full-time staff were needed to edit and distribute it.

The magazine was different from others of those days in that it sought to present a mixture of items. Each issue would contain a number of general, secular articles of interest to young people set alongside those with a direct spiritual challenge.

In 1935, with the magazine well established, Roger sought some way of building on the clear response to *The Pathfinder* and of bringing its readers together. He hit on the idea of running a summer holiday houseparty. He consulted a handbook of private schools and found suitable premises for the month of August at Oldfield School in Swanage in Dorset. Renting the school from August 3rd to the 31st, he persuaded a number of friends to come and help as leaders, including J. B. Phillips, later to become so well known as an author and biblical translator. The holiday was advertised in *The Pathfinder*, offering 'a holiday houseparty for single people under twenty-five'.

This attracted groups from all walks of life. The programme was deliberately not fully organised, but contained all the elements expected of that sort of a holiday – outings, picnics and boat trips, and concluded with a grand concert. One day there was even an air display from Sir Alan Cobham. The houseparty also proved to have a great spiritual impact; not that anyone was forced to attend meetings or the evening epilogues – indeed nothing was regarded as compulsory – but the atmosphere generated by a large group of Christians together on holiday proved very powerful. Some who were nominal Christians discovered the Living Christ for the first time, others rediscovered a purpose for their Christian lives. Away from their homes and their work many of the young people felt free to talk openly about their hopes, needs and fears.

The houseparty had been a great success and was clearly something to be repeated. Two houseparty centres were taken for the summer of the next year and three for the summer of 1937. The running of *The Pathfinder* had become a full-time job and in 1936 Roger left his parochial work in order to concentrate on it. This also enabled him to hire centres and run houseparties at other times of the year. By now Roger was convinced of the powerful means of evangelism provided by holiday houseparties. A new idea began to formulate in his mind: why not have a permanent centre available throughout the year for this work? A few possibilities were explored, but for the moment nothing materialised. By 1939 the total number of people present at summer houseparties had risen to over 800 and the programme of holiday activities with an epilogue each evening was well established.

However, as the war became more and more inevitable, the houseparties of that year were not completed. After only six days, a party at Château d'Oex in Switzerland were advised to return home and caught the last regular express to Paris. At Bodelwyddan Castle in North Wales members of the houseparty began to get telegrams recalling them to work, and by the middle of the second week, the houseparty was badly depleted. On the Thursday everybody went home. The secretary of that houseparty, responsible for arranging the special train to get people away, was an ordinand named Gordon Strutt, and he was to play a very significant part in the next stage in the founding of Lee Abbey.

The outbreak of the war halted the work of *The Path-*

*finder*. A paper shortage meant that the magazine could not
be produced and there seemed at first to be no place for
holiday houseparties in a country at war. Roger had returned to full-time parochial work, as Vicar of Broxbourne
in Hertfordshire, but God was preparing other men with a
similar vision. Gordon Strutt was to bring together the two
men who were to be at the centre of the establishment of
Lee Abbey.

By 1942 Gordon was ordained and a curate at Carlton-in-
the-Willows. One day one of his parishioners asked him to
meet her Uncle Leslie who was staying with her family.

Now in his mid-forties, Leslie Sutton had been through a
very difficult period in his life. Yet that day it was his deep
faith in the living Christ that was most important. Leslie
shared with Gordon his vision for the Church of England
and what he believed God was going to do. Slowly the story
of his life began to emerge, as he spoke with the stammer
which had been with him since childhood. At the age of
thirteen he had committed his life to Christ through the
ministry of the children's evangelist, Hudson Pope. During
the First World War he had been seriously wounded in the
landing at Gallipoli. He was invalided out, as 'an incurable
deaf mute', yet through the prayers of his family, after
eighteen months of silence, he regained his speech. Convinced that God had spared his life for a purpose, he felt
called to the mission field and went out to the Belgian
Congo with what was to become W.E.C. – The Worldwide
Evangelisation Crusade. After only two years, however,
Leslie's health forced him to return to England, where he
became adjutant for the W.E.C. at their Missionary Training Colony in Upper Norwood. Part of the work included
running residential weekend conferences where he saw the
power of Christ at work changing people's lives and equip-
ping them for service both at home and overseas.

At Norwood he became engaged to another member of
the W.E.C. community, Elisabeth Hand, who was responsible for the women candidates. They were both mem-

bers of the Church of England and longed to see what they experienced at W.E.C. becoming part of the life of the Anglican Church, but they could find little sympathy for their Anglican loyalties among their W.E.C. colleagues. So after much prayer, they decided to leave W.E.C. after their marriage, with the specific purpose of starting some work that would seek to bring revival within the Church of England. While dressing for her wedding, Elisabeth noticed for the first time a suspicious lump on her breast. A week later the doctor diagnosed widespread, inoperable cancer. She had to go to hospital straightaway for daily treatment, but after only eight months of marriage she died.

Thus it was a man broken, but undefeated, who talked to Gordon Strutt. And as he spoke, Gordon remembered a letter he had recently received from Roger de Pemberton, who was now the vicar of St. Nicholas' Church in Rochester. The letter had asked if Gordon could suggest anyone who could come and join Roger on the staff at St. Nicholas to work especially amongst men: Gordon sensed that here might be just the man. Leslie Sutton set off to Rochester to visit Roger for the weekend and did not return!

Since Roger de Pemberton had become vicar of St. Nicholas there had been no shortage of activity in the parish, and there was plenty to keep Leslie occupied. The congregation was growing quickly, attracted by the charismatic personality of the vicar and the strong, direct preaching. Roger was a man full of new ideas. A typical example of his enterprise was to hire a top military band to play in the castle grounds, which attracted a large number of people to open-air services. On a summer Sunday evening it was not unknown for 1,200 people to gather to hear the band and also the Gospel. Nor did Roger allow his literary skills to lie dormant. Much of what he had learned in producing *The Pathfinder* was applied to the parish magazine, *The Rochester Review*, and its publication was eagerly awaited by many people who had little contact with

St. Nicholas. As well as the normal parish news, he included many articles similar to those which made *The Pathfinder* so popular.

As the war stretched on into its third year, Roger's thoughts began to turn again to houseparties, and he wondered whether he could recommence the very successful work that had been halted in 1939. He wrote to the Ministry of Labour to try out the idea and received a warm response from their welfare officers. In August 1942 he rented a school in St. Austell, Cornwall and the houseparties were restarted. That season in St. Austell was to have a particular significance for Roger for it was there that he met and fell in love with Peggy Hotblack. They were married at Tiverton in 1943.

Clearly there was a real need for such holiday houseparties during wartime and it was decided to run two further houseparties in August of the next year. St. Austell was booked again and the welfare officers of the Ministry of Labour undertook much of the recruitment. To find another centre, Roger returned to Truman and Knightley's *Guide to Public Schools* which had proved so helpful in finding suitable premises in the past. A supplement in the back of the war-time edition included a list of addresses of all the schools which had been evacuated. It was here that Roger again came across the name of Lee Abbey, Lynton, and memories of that June afternoon, ten years earlier, came flooding back. A letter from the headmaster indicated that the building might be available for use in August and so together with Leslie he went down to inspect the premises.

The intervening ten years had not been kind to Lee Abbey and its estate; it was a very different sight that confronted Roger and Leslie as they inspected the building in the pouring rain.

The main building had been erected by the local squire, Charles Bailey, who had purchased the property in 1841. In keeping with the fashion of that period he had adopted a

Neo-Gothic design for the house including two stone fol-
lies, in the form of ruined towers. Even the name was
adapted to the spirit of the age and the Lee Manor of Lorna
Doone became the more stately Lee Abbey.

In due course the estate passed to his son, but on his
death in 1919 it was divided up and the house with 360 acres
was purchased by a hotel company. With great enthusiasm
they enlarged the accommodation by building a new bedroom wing, and laid out a golf course, but this was not an
easy time for such a smart hotel, set in a relatively remote
part of the country. The economic situation soon meant
that little money could be spent on the fabric of the
building, and the declaration of war set the seal on the fate
of the company: it went bankrupt. The Official Receivers,
into whose hands Lee Abbey then passed had little difficulty in finding a use for the building. It was the start of the
blitz and many boarding schools in the south-east, their
own buildings commandeered by the Army, were looking
for accommodation to which they could evacuate their
pupils. The West Country was an obvious area and there
was some competition to acquire suitable premises. So it
was at the time of Dunkirk in June 1940 that Brambletye
Preparatory School from East Grinstead in Sussex moved
their pupils, furniture, equipment, and all that remained of
their teaching and domestic staff to take up residence in
Lee Abbey.

It was now a very dilapidated house that Roger and
Leslie visited. The building which had looked so impressive
in 1932 was completely daubed with camouflage, lest any
German bombers returning down the Bristol Channel from
raids over Bristol, might choose to jettison their remaining
bombs on a prominent building. The octagonal room, built
as a music room by Charles Bailey and subsequently used as
the hushed lounge of the smart hotel, was now the noisy
dining room for 100 small boys. The fine bedrooms, their
carpets gone, were dormitories; the golf course had disappeared under grass and weeds; and the café on the beach

had fallen victim to vandals. Yet they were not deterred. An arrangement was made with the headmaster to rent the house for the following August and for the first time a holiday houseparty was advertised for Lee Abbey at the cost of £2.10s. per week.

As today, Lee Abbey proved to be an ideal setting for a holiday. There were plenty of opportunities for walks, either on the numerous paths within the estate or on the coastal path to Hunter's Inn with its magnificent view, or perhaps further afield up on to Exmoor; Lee Bay provided a safe beach from which to swim; there was a tennis court; for those who just wanted to be lazy, there was a lawn at the front of the house from which to take in the magnificent view, and above all it was peaceful.

But the living conditions were primitive even by war-time standards. The only furniture in the house belonged to the school so most people slept in dormitories with two or three others, on beds which were designed for young boys! Many people came down in the mornings complaining of aching limbs and the lumps in the mattresses! The locks on the bathroom doors had long since disappeared, and there was quite a lot of truth in the rumours that rats had been seen around the store-sheds in the inner courtyard and that there were cockroaches in the kitchen. All the guests were expected to share in domestic duties, washing up, laying tables, preparing vegetables and serving meals, and this was all considered to be part of the fun of the holiday.

As with his other houseparties, this first holiday at Lee Abbey was run by a team of committed Christians invited by Roger from among his many contacts. They came as guests but arranged the programme and were responsible for the pastoral care of all the visitors. Each day concluded with the epilogue, not the brief talk with which that word is often associated today, but a full-length session in which the claims of Christ were clearly presented. This proved again to be a holiday in which many people took a decisive step in their Christian lives. A couple of letters from *The*

*Rochester Review* in 1944 give an impression of the impact that Lee Abbey holidays were making.

> It was the first real break that I had had for five years and there was God right in the middle of the team, reaching out and touching each one of us, either directly or indirectly. My own experience was one of drawing closer to God and the marvel of His prevailing love. One day while we walked to Watersmeet, at one point the water dropped suddenly over a smoothly flattened rock, about three or four feet – the rocks behind at the side were rough and scratchy – and the thought passed through my mind: 'If only we would let God's love flow over us so the rough patches would be smoothed out and His love would flow out to the other lives that we meet daily.'

> Now that I am back at home and beginning to settle down into ordinary life once more, I can see more than ever of what God has done for me. My whole range of ideas and ideals seemed to have changed from a good but completely shallow point of view, to one in which it all seems a waste of time if one has not found the great secret of knowing God.

It was decided to use Lee Abbey again for houseparties the following August, but already Roger was getting another idea.

# 2

## Starting Out

When Leslie Sutton joined Roger de Pemberton at Rochester, he brought with him a deep yearning in his heart to see revival come to the Church of England. He knew that prayer changed things and he believed that revival would come only as people prayed. This was his constant theme and he practised what he preached. For almost two years Leslie and Roger with a few others prayed for the revival of the Church.

Their deep concern was being felt in many other quarters. The war had revealed the spiritual poverty of the Church of England. The great movement of population caused by conscription and evacuation revealed just how formal and hollow much British religion had become. Army Chaplains discovered through their 'Padre's Hours' how few of their men had any real grasp of the Christian message. For the first time a religious Public Opinion Poll had been taken, organised by Mass Observation. Its conclusions were published under the title 'Puzzled People'; it revealed that the majority of the nation had no Christian belief and that even many Church people did not accept some of the fundamentals of the Christian faith – that Jesus was the Son of God or that He had risen from the dead. It was already clear that a massive task was going to face the Church if it were to regain contact with the general population after the war.

It is often said that the Church of England's answer to any problem is to appoint a committee! On this occasion

William Temple, the Archbishop of Canterbury, was fully aware of the seriousness and challenge of the situation. As early as 1943 he called together a Commission to 'survey the whole problem of modern evangelism', so that the Church might have a clear strategy when the war was over. It was a diverse group of fifty men and women who met together for the first time in February 1944 in the Jerusalem Chamber of Westminster Abbey. At that time the differences between the Evangelicals and Anglo-Catholics were considerably more pronounced than they are today and so this group – which was chosen to be representative of the whole Church, so that it could speak to the whole Church – encompassed a wide spectrum of theological opinion. Yet all shared a special concern and interest in evangelism.

The findings of the Commission were not to be published until the end of the war. The report was clear in its conclusions and did not mince words, even in the title itself: *Towards the Conversion of England*. Thirty-five years later it still makes challenging reading, as it analyses 'a wholesale drift from organised religion'. It concludes that the Church has become irrelevant to the life and thought of the community in general, demonstrated by the widespread decline in church-going and the collapse of Christian moral standards.

The message comes over clearly:

The aim of evangelism is conversion. Conversion is the reorientation of life from self to God through Jesus Christ. Conversion may be sudden . . . or conversion may be gradual . . . But whether sudden or gradual, it is the birthright of every child of God to be converted . . .

We cannot expect to get far with evangelism until three facts are faced. First, the vast majority of English people need to be converted to Christianity. Secondly, a large number of Church people also require to be converted, in the sense of their possessing that personal knowledge of Christ which can be ours only by the dedication of the whole self, whatever the cost. Thirdly, such personal knowledge of Christ is the only satisfactory basis for testimony to others . . .

It will thus be realised that the really daunting feature of modern evangelism is not the masses of population to be converted, but that most of the worshipping community are only half converted.

The report did not merely analyse problems; it contained many practical suggestions. The key to evangelism, it suggested, was the clergy who traditionally had been trained to be pastors rather than evangelists. Training in evangelism was desperately needed.

For such a situation the paramount necessity is that the parish clergy as a body should gain a new vision, fresh hope and a Baptism of the Holy Spirit. Any forward move, therefore, in evangelism must begin with the clergy themselves, and with their coming together to gain a new liberation into the vision of the Glory of God.

The next urgent need described by the report was for the mobilisation and training of the laity for evangelism. 'The Apostolate of the Laity' had to be rediscovered, not merely theologically, but practically. Among many suggestions the idea was put forward of small groups of laity being trained in a parish to go out as a mission team to other places.

The report's publication in 1945, dedicated to William Temple, who had died in 1944, was welcomed by many within the Church who felt that it reinforced their own conviction that God was calling for a great revival. However, to the main body of the Church of England such suggestions were too revolutionary, and many chose to 'leave it for future debate' and so forget all about it.

As so often happens when God is at work, even before the Commission had its first meeting, Roger de Pemberton had been thinking along similar lines. Roger was asked

to serve as one of the members of the Commission. Moreover, Christopher Chevasse, Bishop of Rochester, was
appointed as chairman, and he lived very near to Roger and
Leslie in Rochester.

It was during the first houseparty at Lee Abbey in 1943,
over a cup of coffee at the Tea Cottage, that Roger talked
about his thoughts for the future of Lee Abbey with one of
the team. This latest scheme was very simple; he wanted to
buy the place as a centre for evangelism. His pre-war
experience had convinced him of the value of holiday
houseparties as a means of evangelism and Christian training. The headmaster of the school had indicated to him that
as soon as the war ended, the school would be returning to
Sussex and the property would be up for sale. Its poor state
and the fact that few people would be interested in such a
large property meant that it would be cheap. Here was a
great opportunity to launch out into something entirely
new in the Church of England – a permanent centre for
evangelism.

Roger's enthusiasm for the scheme was not immediately
shared. Where would the money come from for the down
payment on the mortgage, let alone the purchase price? Did
he realise that he was thinking of buying a building that was
virtually derelict? Was it really likely that there would be
sufficient people willing to come to houseparties throughout the summer months? Who was going to run the place?
The hotel had gone bankrupt; he might end up the same
way.

However, on his return to Rochester he continued to
pursue this goal of purchasing Lee Abbey. The headmaster
of the school was keen on the idea and even agreed to buy
the property himself and in turn sell it to Roger. This would
guarantee a lower price for Roger, since the headmaster
was the sitting tenant; it would also release the school from
any responsibility for damage to the property during their
tenancy.

Roger began to circulate a nine-page document among

some of his friends. After explaining his own experience of running holiday houseparties, he spelt out his proposal to purchase Lee Abbey. For five months each year from May to September it could be used as a permanent houseparty centre. In the winter months it might become a training college in evangelism – a place where laity and clergy could come for training in Christian work, Bible study etc. Possible developments for the estate were also mooted – the building of summer chalets; the hire of beach huts; a camping site on one of the golf courses; a car park open to the public; a swimming pool at the top of the beach to use when the tide was out. The property would be held by a trust and registered as a charity. The organisation would also be administered by the Trustees who, in the main, would be those engaged in the work.

A vast amount of work was necessary for the purchase of the property – the securing of loans and the setting up of a charity – and as this was begun, a group of people began to come together, convinced that this apparently foolhardy scheme might indeed have the hand of God upon it. As Roger shared the proposal with his contacts, it seemed to be offering exactly the spearhead for evangelism and training that many were convinced was desperately needed. Together they began to pray to discover whether this was the will of God. If it were of God, they knew that it would succeed; if not, it would fail – there were certainly plenty of things that could confound the purchase.

One obvious problem was the lack of money. It was not until the basic commitment to purchase had been made that Roger received a letter from a firm of London solicitors. He opened it to learn that a second cousin of his had died and he had been left £6,000, which he offered as a loan for the mortgage down-payment. God was indeed at work.

August 1944 saw the second year of holiday houseparties for war workers at Lee Abbey. Yet few of the guests, as they were swimming or playing tennis, knew that indoors the first meeting was taking place to draw up the legal documents necessary for the purchase of the property. On October 18th the Pathfinder Trust came into being, with seven men responsible for the oversight of its work – Cuthbert Bardsley (Provost of Southwark); Jack Winslow (Chaplain of Bryanston School); Geoffrey Rogers (Candidates Secretary of C.M.S.); Oswald Garrard (a vicar from Bedford); Derek Wigram (a house-master from Bryanston School); together with Leslie Sutton as Secretary and Roger himself as chairman they became the Trustees of the Pathfinder Trust and Council of Management of the Pathfinder Fellowship. Each had been carefully chosen by Roger, for he was anxious not only that they should fully share his own vision for evangelism and lay training, but also that they should be representative of the different recognised groups within the Church. For instance, Jack Winslow was well known as an Anglo-Catholic and Derek Wigram had many contacts with conservative evangelicals. A third influence that was to be significant in the early days of Lee Abbey was the Oxford Group later to become Moral Rearmament. Both Jack Winslow and Cuthbert Bardsley had once been closely associated with the group but becoming increasingly unhappy with certain features of its teaching they had left it. Then, as now, Lee Abbey aimed to serve the whole Church, rather than being identified with any one particular group.

The first task of the Trustees was to approve the arrangements made by Roger for the purchase of the property and the raising of the necessary money. The total cost was £28,000.

As England entered the final year of the war, arrangements went steadily ahead for the purchase of Lee Abbey. For the first time an Easter houseparty was held, followed by a week of prayer and preparation for evangelism. About sixty people attended and it attracted the wide range of Christian experience that had been hoped for, but tensions were apparent, especially among those who were anxious about the influence of the Oxford Group. If Lee Abbey were going to be an Oxford Group Centre, then many other people would not be associated with it; this suspicion was to dog Lee Abbey in its first years. In August two fortnightly houseparties were arranged at Lee Abbey and Roger had also taken over Allhallows, Rousdon, a school near Lyme Regis. There was a further fortnight designed especially as a holiday training course in evangelism. With their own building now vacated by the Army, the school was ready to return to Sussex. As the houseparty ended the removal vans moved in and so on September 8th, 1945, Lee Abbey finally became the property of the Pathfinder Trust.

# 3

# The First Year

What a task confronted Leslie Sutton as the furniture vans moved off down the Valley of Rocks. It had already been agreed that as soon as the school vacated the premises Leslie should move from Rochester and take up permanent residence at Lee Abbey as acting Warden. Now, with a few volunteer helpers, mainly staying on from the houseparty, he surveyed the vast empty building. Where should they begin?

It is not easy for the person familiar with Lee Abbey today, with its central heating, double-glazed windows and wall-to-wall carpeting, to imagine the state of the building. The last two years of the school's occupation had done nothing to improve things. There were broken windows to repair and inspection underneath the floor-boards revealed that much of the wiring was charred and urgently needed replacing. Rats and mice had taken up occupation and above all the place was filthy. In the back yard piles of rubbish, accumulated by the hotel and school, had to be shifted. All this was made more difficult by the acute shortage of tools and building materials at the end of the war.

The building also needed furnishing. Furniture, cooking utensils and crockery were needed for some 150 people, and they had nothing. However, as the needs became known, many gifts came in, including clothing coupons which were exchanged for curtain material. Leslie and his helpers visited nearly every auction within a seventy-mile radius of Lynton to find beds, mattresses, chairs, etc. Meanwhile, in Rochester, Roger and Peggy had returned to live in the vicarage when it had been de-requisitioned by the Army, and one of the nissen huts that had been erected in the garden became a furniture repository as Roger visited sales to obtain furniture from some of the wartime societies, as they began to close down.

A further problem was the water and electricity supplies. The estate was too remote to be connected to the mains, but a number of springs produced a very pure supply of drinking water for the house. They also provided the power to drive a Pelton Wheel, which was housed near the beach and generated the electricity for the lighting. The school had encountered enormous problems with this, for if the water was too low, or the springs became clogged with leaves, then the lights would flicker, fade and often go out altogether. It was clearly going to be necessary to augment the supply with the diesel generator installed by the hotel company but which had hardly been used. This particular incident was to provide Leslie with one of his favourite illustrations for epilogues:

'One morning Bert the gardener took me to a big double door in the "annexe" regions in the back yard. "Thur be an engine in thur, zur" he said.

'We opened it up, but all we could see was a pile of old junk: bedsteads, mattresses, broken mirrors, torn rolls of carpet, discarded kitchen utensils – all thrown in a great tangled heap.

'Bert still insisted "thur be an engine underneath", and as we pulled out the rubbish it came into view – a Rushton and Hornby diesel engine which should have been providing light and power for all the house.

'Then men set to work and cleaned and oiled it till it shone, filled its tank with oil, and when all was done two of them grasped the handles of the starting-lever and struggled to turn the wheel.

'The engine gave a few hesitating chuffs and then stopped dead. So we wrote to the maker, and he sent us a beautifully illustrated book. This showed us in every detail how the engine should work.

'We carefully followed all the instructions, and tried again. This time there were just a few more chuffs . . . and then silence once again. We knew something was radically wrong. There was nothing more we could do to make the engine work. So once more we wrote to the maker, and this time he sent a man, his own representative, one who had been with the firm from boyhood and knew these engines from A to Z – George, a little bowler-hatted Yorkshireman.

'He lived with us, and got straight down to work. He soon found that the main crank shaft was out of true, and he put in a new one. When he was satisfied that all was in order, and with all our men standing round watching, he connected the engine to the pressure bottle, pulled over the automatic starting-lever, and lo! the big wheel began to turn, slowly at first, but soon settling down to its right rhythm. And the lights came on in the house. Then George, black to the elbows in oil, folded his arms and stood back regarding it lovingly, and said, "Ow I loves to 'ear 'em 'um!"'

As the winter progressed, God began to bring together the people needed to run Lee Abbey in its first season. From the beginning it was seen as imperative that those who came to work at any job should be committed Christians, coming because they believed that they were called by God to share in this new work. A Church Army Captain, John Ellis, was appointed as Estate Manager with the massive task of overseeing the 350-acre estate that had suffered as badly as the building. Slowly other posts were filled: secretary, housekeeper, mechanic, cook/caterer, gardeners. In the early hours of June 1st, 1946, the last load of furniture arrived and later that day the opening house-party began. Although the house was now furnished and was habitable, it was going to take a very long time to repair the building thoroughly and reclaim the estate.

'An opening Conference and Dedication for those actively interested in Evangelism and Lee Abbey' was the title for this first week at Pentecost 1946. It was a great gathering including many of the people who had been drawn into this new vision for evangelism over the previous couple of years. Rain fell steadily for most of the week but Thursday, June 5th, the day set aside for the Dedication, dawned a glorious, sunny day. The service took the form of a procession with the Bishop of Exeter, Dr. Charles Curzon, the Archdeacon of Barnstaple, many local clergy, the Trustees and conference guests. Singing hymns, the procession wound its way round the building, outside and in, stopping to dedicate the land, the workshops, the Chapel and the octagonal lounge.

Roger, as chairman of the Trustees, outlined the events that had led up to that day:

'It was all prayer and faith, and so, please God, it will continue. We are yet in the dark as to a good deal, and yet in considerable need as to a good deal, but we are convinced that where God guides, God provides, and we have not the slightest hesitation in saying that our needs in personnel, in materials, and in finance, will be provided.'

There were three things he believed that Lee Abbey should do:

'First, by trying as well as we can in our small way to stir the Church to a greater concern for evangelism, which many of us believe is its primary concern and responsibility today; secondly, to call men and women into an experience of radical conversion. We believe, quite emphatically, that human nature is diseased; that in some way it needs recreating by turning to God through faith in Christ, which brings about a change in life, and regeneration . . . thirdly, we are much concerned with the whole question of Christian leadership. One of the things the Church is suffering from is the lack of creative Christian leadership on the part of the laity.'

Cuthbert Bardsley, Provost of Southwark, was next to speak in an address that was to prove prophetic both for the nation and for Lee Abbey. As he analysed the needs of the modern world he spoke of two great faiths striving against each other. These were Christianity and Communism, of which he said:

'It is a militant faith spreading fast, and it may present one of the greatest challenges to Christianity that it has ever been called upon to face. Against that there is only one alternative, and that is a militant, vital Christianity with its passionate belief in a future life and victorious moral power, and with its grand past history so often forgotten.'

Two things were needed for the modern world. Firstly, 'the creation of confessed and confessing Christians, men and women whose hearts the Lord has touched, who have working experience of the forgiveness and love of Jesus Christ, who know the authority of the Word "Thus saith the Lord", and who are able intelligently to introduce other people to the saving grace of Christ.' The second need was to have not merely lone-wolf Christians, but teams; 'an atom force of spiritual energy that nothing can resist'.

'The Church congregation is often too large a unit for the Spirit to work through effectively. The congregation needs to have at the heart of it a number of cells of dynamic united love.'

He concluded, 'There needs to come into the Church a new fighting spirit. There is too much depression about today – too much lack of faith. We have lost faith because so many others have not gone far enough to find faith. It is my passionate belief that Lee Abbey will recover for thousands their faith in God, and will raise the morale of Church and State to militant, pentecostal Christianity.'

Any visitor present at Lee Abbey on that momentous day, watching the procession and listening to the speeches, would have had no doubts about Lee Abbey's close links with the Church of England. The vast majority of people present were Anglicans and the diocesan Bishop of Exeter led the service. Lee Abbey had been founded by Anglicans and its stated purpose was to seek the specific renewal of the Church of England. Yet the Trustees were extremely anxious from the beginning that Lee Abbey should remain independent of the Church of England establishment, because they did not want its vision frustrated by the inevitable bureaucracy of Church committees. Thus Lee Abbey has never received any direct financial support from Church of England funds.

Today Lee Abbey is Anglican in that the Warden and Chaplains are members of the Church of England and the worship uses Church of England service books, yet the aim has shifted over the years. Lee Abbey now seeks to serve the whole of the Church in England, though not from a non-denominational stand-point. Members of the Community come from a wide span of denominations from Roman Catholic to Brethren, and in the same way it is hoped that all the guests who come to stay will feel equally welcomed and at home whatever their denomination or church background.

Between June and the end of September in that first season five holiday houseparties were held, and some 600 people visited Lee Abbey. With the International Houseparty and 'Houseparty for Younger Married Couples and Children under eight years', a successful pattern was established which would be repeated in many succeeding years. Although guests enjoyed the comfort of full-length beds, it was still necessary to ask for help with domestic duties on a rota basis. Many new friendships were forged over the great deep wooden sinks, or 'spud-bashing' in the inner courtyard. The practice of previous years was followed, with leadership taken by specially invited guest speakers, who were responsible for the epilogues. Each houseparty had a number of guests who had attended a previous houseparty and were committed Christians. From them a small team was selected who would meet together each day to pray for the houseparty and share together any problems.

As the letters came back from guests, there was no doubt that the Holy Spirit had been doing much during that first summer. There was the young man who after his conversion declared 'It's just like being born again,' with no knowledge that he was using the very words of Jesus Himself. There was a vicar from the Midlands who had been sent to find out what Lee Abbey was like; he discovered that he was not right with God, entered into a new commitment and went back to bear witness to his Diocesan committee. At one houseparty no fewer than thirty young people professed conversion.

Throughout this period Leslie Sutton had been acting as Warden, but the intention had always been that there should be a permanent pastoral staff at Lee Abbey to run the houseparties and conferences. A long time was spent at the July meeting of the Council of Management discussing the post of Warden, with the result that Roger was appointed as Warden, Leslie Sutton as sub-warden and the Rev. J. H. (Tommy) Thompson as Chaplain. Tommy Thompson had joined Roger the previous year in Rochester as associate vicar. So on October 24th the de Pembertons and Thompsons arrived and Roger took up his new post as the first Warden of Lee Abbey.

# 4

# *Life Together*

The re-emergence of communities of Christians, living and sharing their lives together, has been a marked feature of the Church in the last thirty years. Experiments in establishing communities have ranged from large schemes involving hundreds of people to small groups of four or five living together in 'extended households'. The majority of people living in such communities have gone into the venture with little idea of what it involves. While some schemes have folded after only a short time, others have matured as they have evolved. Few people would claim that it has been easy, and most find themselves facing unexpected physical, emotional and spiritual demands.

The reasons behind this widespread interest in community life are complex.

There is a feeling among many Christians that the Church has become too remote and institutionalised, with members coming into contact with their fellow-believers only at worship for an hour on Sunday, and possibly for one mid-week evening activity. There is a deep desire to return to a style of life closer to that of the early Christians in the days of the Acts of the Apostles.

However, a number of secular communities have also come into being within the last few years; these are often centred upon some political or social ideal. This desire for community living is not difficult to understand in a society where increasing numbers of people lack any experience of close family relationships and where loneliness is now acknowledged to be a major problem.

In the winter of 1946–7 those whom God had brought together at Lee Abbey began to work out their relationships but at that time they knew virtually nothing about community life. Indeed it was almost by accident that they discovered they were a community, and had to work out the implications. At the dedication, Cuthbert Bardsley had talked about the powerful impact of a group of witnessing Christians. It soon became clear that in the establishment of Lee Abbey as a centre for evangelism, God's plan was not concerned merely with the restoration of a large Victorian house; He was also building a community of people. Guests have continued to testify over the years that what made the greatest impact upon them when visiting Lee Abbey was not the glorious scenery of North Devon, or the house or the opportunity of getting away from the pressures of their normal life, but to witness the life of the Community, living and working together. After thirty-five years the members of the Community still find that very hard to believe!

For centuries the religious communities had played an important part in the life of the Church of England, and a definite pattern was assumed to be basic for anyone living 'the religious life'. It involved a convent or monastery with a single-sex community normally following the Rule of Life laid down by one of the great Saints like Francis or Benedict. Many such communities were refounded as a result of the great Anglo-Catholic Revival in the nineteenth century, and evangelical Christians were often suspicious of the idea of a community because of these 'Catholic' overtones. The idea that Lee Abbey, with its mixed group of lay people, could be a religious community was hard to grasp. One Church dignitary is reputed to have commented that he didn't approve of 'monks and nuns living together'.

Though the size of the Lee Abbey Community has

greatly increased, so that it now comprises about fifty-five adults, the basic principles of Community membership have not altered since the first year. The Community is made up of men and women covering a wide age range; they are mainly single but there are always several families (six at the time of writing) some with children.

At the beginning there were two distinct groups: the permanent and the temporary Community. The former, like Roger and Leslie, were those called by God from different spheres of work to serve at Lee Abbey for an indefinite period. At this time the Lord was bringing together a team of people, many of whom were to stay for a number of years. Madeleine Wheen was to stay as Lady Warden for twenty-eight years, and at the time of writing Ursula Kay and Pat Pilditch have each been members of the Community for over twenty years and Edna Madgwick has been a member of the estate team for thirty-one years. Long-term members are essential in order to maintain continuity and stability, yet Community membership at Lee Abbey has never been regarded as a life-long commitment, but as one part, albeit very significant, of any person's life.

Many Community members will stay for about one to two years, with others coming for just a few months to help during the busy summer season.

It is not always easy to find the stable, able-bodied Christian men and women who are needed for the ministry at Lee Abbey. The Lee Abbey Community is no place for a person to come to try and escape from his problems or to find a cushy job. As well as their basic work in one of the departments – house, kitchen, office and estate – Community members are expected to spend time with the guests, being prepared to chat at meals, over coffee or after the epilogue in the evenings. As the body of Christ is made up of many different parts, so in the Lee Abbey Community God brings together a group of people from diverse backgrounds. Many are people who have trained for a profession: teachers, nurses, social workers, secretaries and accountants. There have often been several who are preparing for ordination or for missionary service overseas, and a number spend a year in the Community before going to college, or beginning a new course of training. Others come to Lee Abbey with a whole range of practical experience to offer to the life of the Community, farming, catering, engineering, gardening etc. It is fascinating to witness the way that God honours His promises and meets the need of the Community; often a particular skill is not discovered until the person has actually joined!

For many people a time at Lee Abbey has been one when they have received a call to a particular sphere of full-time Christian ministry – ordination, missionary service and sometimes to become members of the traditional communities. Few members have found life in the Community easy; after that first winter Leslie wrote in the *Lee Abbey Review* 'team work and living in Community is a testing and strengthening experience. It is costly to our individual pride of self-will because each must work as part of the whole and be open to the criticism and advice of others.' Yet the experience has proved enormously enriching even though at the time it might be painful.

One great example from these early days was 'Pop' Hughes, a retired Wiltshire farmer. He came to Lee Abbey in 1946 when his daughter, Betty, was appointed as head cook. They lived together at Lower Lodge and Pop was asked to look after the farm and the gardens. So each day he would drive up the hill in his pony-cart drawn by 'Dolly'. Many found him extremely difficult; he did not seem to fit in at all, and he often used to wave his stick and shout at people. Yet as the years went by the Holy Spirit was mellowing Pop, so that when it was time for him to retire from outdoor work it was found that he had a very real pastoral ministry. He would spend much of his time sitting in the small lounge writing letters, or on one of the seats outside just chatting with anyone who came along. Countless people would testify to the enormous help they had received from Pop, in his new God-given role as a grandfatherly counsellor. In 1955 Betty moved on from Lee Abbey but Pop remained until his death in 1960.

Another notable feature of the Community since its beginning is that there has been a constant supply of members from overseas. On the Saturday after he had moved in, Roger set off on a tour of the continent, which included a visit to the Ecumenical Centre at Bossey in Switzerland and also to Holland and France. As well as encouraging many people to come to the International Houseparty, he was recruiting for the Community and in March two Swiss boys arrived at Lee Abbey. By the next year there were no fewer than eight overseas Community members – four from Holland, one from Denmark and three from Norway – and they were to be the first of a whole succession who have made valuable contributions to the life of the Community. Indeed, in the early years it would have been almost impossible to staff the house without these overseas members. However, the presence of the European Community members brought a great deal of pain. Memories of the war were still very fresh; Dutch and German girls living closely together created very real tensions to which the healing, reconciling power of Christ had to be brought.

Central to the life of any Christian Community must be worship together. 'Common life under the Word', wrote Bonhoeffer, 'begins with common worship at the beginning of the day.' It is only in time spent together waiting on God, listening to His Word, sharing in adoration, thanksgiving, and intercession, that a Community will receive the strength it needs. Yet even for a group of Christians who live together under the same roof, this is something which has to be jealously guarded if it is not to be eroded by the many 'top-priority' activities that demand attention.

The Community met together at the beginning of the first winter season in 1946 to work out a pattern of worship which it hoped would be expressive of the life of the whole Community, representing, as it did, a very wide spectrum of tradition. There was the need to combine the formal and informal, and leave room for experimentation and the flexibility to adapt as things worked out. They formulated a structure including Holy Communion, Evensong, Bible meditation, daily intercessions and informal prayer.

In the end a very much simpler pattern was adopted and this has changed little over the years. For thirty-five minutes at the beginning of each day, except Sunday, there are community prayers, which all members of the Community are expected to attend unless they are taking their day off. The format varies from day to day and is determined by the members of the Community who take it in turns to lead the worship – the only mandatory items are a prescribed Bible passage and a time for extemporary 'open' prayer. One day each week is earmarked as Community Day which begins with a corporate Communion service. Experience has proved that it is essential to have a day when the whole Community can be together. One of the questions put to those wishing to become full Community members is, 'Do you intend to make the weekly corporate Communion the central act of your work and worship?' It is this service that lies at the heart of the life of the Lee Abbey Community.

Community life offers plenty of other opportunities for prayer together in smaller groups. Once a week, with the other members of their department, each Community member shares in community intercessions, a time set aside to pray for some of the many specific needs for which people request Lee Abbey to pray. In addition several departments set a short time each day to share in informal prayer together. On most Sunday mornings there will be a service of Holy Communion with the guests, and there are many other occasions for worship in the programme arranged each week for visitors.

The first winter in the Community underlined the very

considerable material sacrifice which God required of those whom He brought to Lee Abbey. Each member received their board and keep together with a personal allowance, which varied according to circumstances but was sometimes as little as ten shillings a week. However, as the winter progressed with no income from guests, Lee Abbey's financial situation became so serious that many were not even receiving this small amount. At one time logs were chopped up from the many fallen trees in the woods and sold to the coal merchant in Lynton in order to bring in some money.

Living conditions were also far from easy. There was very little privacy, and nearly everybody had to share a room with one or two others. It was also generally believed that no Community member had a bed with a spring in it! The weather added to the difficulties; 1946–7 proved to be the hardest winter for over fifty years. In one way Lee Abbey was spared many problems as there was no shortage of wood on the estate for fuel, and they were generating their own electricity. However, the long spell of snow meant that many vital jobs could not be done. The house was cut off from the outside world for quite a time, and the only way of getting essential supplies was by taking a sledge 1¼ miles through the drifts to Lynton. A further hindrance to work occurred with an outbreak of 'flu that managed to lay low nearly the whole Community.

It was not easy to get guests to stay at Lee Abbey during the winter, but thirty people did book in for a ten-day Christmas houseparty, which proved a very happy occasion. On Christmas morning everyone was wakened by a group walking round the house singing carols. At tea-time Father Christmas, in the form of Pop, arrived with a present for each guest and Christmas dinner was eaten by candlelight.

For many this Christmas was to be much more than just a jolly time to forget about the problems of the world. Many guests were touched by the Holy Spirit during those ten days. Among them was Rachel, a Jewish girl who had come with a friend. The friend, who was a radiant Christian, was a refugee from Germany who had seen both her parents killed, but had seen such proof of a 'faith that works' in the home to which she had been allocated, that she had become a Christian. Rachel had agreed to come with her to Lee Abbey for a holiday, but with the understanding that she would definitely not attend 'any religious meeting'! Yet as she became caught up in the festivities of Christmas, she discovered that the baby whose birth the world was celebrating was indeed her own Messiah.

The hardships of the first year had been expected, but in many ways 1947 was to be a much more difficult year for Lee Abbey. Delayed by the fuel crisis, the brochure was sent out very late. This meant that there were far fewer bookings for houseparties than there had been previously. The appalling winter also meant that fewer people were going on holiday and this general slump in the holiday trade hit Lee Abbey. It was a very disturbing situation, both because of its financial implications and because it seemed to thwart the whole purpose of the place. Further problems arose when Tommy Thompson, the Chaplain, resigned in the middle of the summer necessitating a rearrangement of the winter plans. Despite all the discouragements, however, there was a real sense of excitement, because they were involved in the work of God.

Plenty of people outside thought that Lee Abbey could not possibly succeed: it was a waste of time to try to restore this huge building; it would only be a matter of time before they would go bankrupt and have to give it up. Yet the Community knew differently; they were there because God had called them, and because He had called them He was not going to fail them. Theirs was the pioneering spirit.

# 5

## *Personalities*

'It really is extraordinary,' said one English lady to another at an Indian Club, 'he sits on the floor with all these natives eating chapatis and other queer things, all with his fingers; and the amazing thing is that he's an Eton man.' However, the other lady mistook 'Eton' for 'eaten', held up her hands in horror and exclaimed 'Has he!' In those days nothing was too bad to be believed of a man who 'went native'.

The man who had so horrified the English ladies was Jack Winslow, who in May 1948 arrived as Chaplain of Lee Abbey. With the departure of Tommy Thompson, the Council was anxious to find a man from the Anglo-Catholic tradition, who could maintain the balance of church-manship and who shared their vision for evangelism. Jack Winslow was the obvious choice. He had been involved with Lee Abbey from the beginning as one of the Trustees, and had been a frequent speaker at houseparties; moreover he would soon be completing his appointment as Chaplain of Bryanston School in Dorset.

He was already sixty-five years old when he joined the Community, and few people could have imagined that he was to stay for fifteen years. He brought with him to Lee Abbey, not merely the wisdom of age, but also a vast wealth of experience culled from a remarkable ministry.

His father was Rector of Hanworth in Middlesex, and he often wrote of his deep gratitude to God for his childhood spent in that Victorian rectory with his four sisters. He went to school at Eton, where with his fellows he serenaded

Queen Victoria at Windsor Castle for her Diamond Jubilee, and later as a member of the Volunteer Corps was to line the route at her funeral service in St. George's Chapel. After going to Balliol College, Oxford, he was ordained and then went out to India with the Society for the Propagation of the Gospel. However, he found life as a European missionary in India frustrating, and so on returning to India from his first leave, he gathered together a group of young Indian Christians and together they founded a small community. It was called an Ashram and there Indians and Europeans shared a common life of a simple Indian character, with no distinction of race or class, wearing Indian dress and living on a common fund. Through this Ashram many Indians of both high and low caste came to faith in Christ.

In his book *A Testament of Thanksgiving*, Jack Winslow described an experience in September 1932 that he always looked upon as a turning-point in his life. He had been asked to help lead a convention for Christians to be held at Jaffna in Sri Lanka (then called Ceylon). On the long journey from Poona to Ceylon he read a book written by a member of the Oxford Group. It impressed him deeply and made him aware of his own personal pride.

I came to Jaffna and the convention began. A large crowd, mostly of Tamils, filled the old Dutch church evening by evening. About the fifth day it seemed right to give an opportunity for any who so wished to stake out a definite decision for Christ. I had given the address and suggested a time of silence in which we faced what such a decision might mean. In the silence there came to me a strong urge, which I could only interpret as a divine command, to stand up in the pulpit where I was and tell the congregation that I myself needed to lead the way in making a deeper surrender of my own life to God, mentioning some of the things which I had seen were holding me up. It was not easy. After all, I was there to instruct others, as the leader of the convention. But nothing less would have brought the needed humbling of pride.

After I had said my bit, I invited all those who were prepared to face the cost of all-out commitment to stay behind after the service. Some hundreds stayed. We decided to do nothing hurriedly or under stress of emotion, but to give a day's thought to all that such commitment involved. The next night a large number solemnly took their stand for Christ, some for the first time, some in a deeper dedication . . .

I myself made a fuller dedication of my life than ever before. It was a renewal of the very real commitment which I had made at my ordination, but on the deeper level which twenty-five years' experience made possible. The results were astonishing. I awoke the next morning to a new world. New life had flowed into me. I felt as if I had been reborn . . .

But the most significant thing which was given to me on that day was a new outgoing love for people. It is something I find difficult to describe. I had been till then unduly introspective and full of self-concern. I would not say that this has ever entirely vanished, but I did find from Jaffna onwards a new interest in, and care for, the people I met, which introduced me to a richness of fellowship which I had not known before. This was a wonderful gift to me. It was so obviously none of my doing. It was a sheer miracle.[1]

On returning to England Jack served on the Commission that produced *Towards the Conversion of England*, being asked to give the opening devotional session. In June 1940 the BBC had invited him to broadcast a series of three morning services and he received some 10,000 letters in response to what he said.

[1] J. C. Winslow, *A Testament of Thanksgiving* (Hodder & Stoughton, 1974)

In bringing Jack Winslow to Lee Abbey, the Lord was providing a person who was to prove very important both in the growth of the Community, and in ministering to literally thousands of guests.

In 1948 God was drawing together several people who were to work together as a team for the next twelve years. On New Year's Eve Phyllis Lewis arrived to become Assistant Secretary, and soon also first Secretary of the Friends of Lee Abbey. It was not long before Community members began to notice something about Phyllis – she was clearly in love with Leslie Sutton. Phyllis and Leslie were the first of many couples who have been brought together by God through their membership of the Community. At the end of the houseparty season in September, they were married in Lynton Parish Church with a fine reception in the octagonal lounge.

Jack Winslow joined the Community in April, and one week later Madeleine Wheen arrived. It was in 1945 that a friend had persuaded her to organise the catering for the August houseparties at Allhallows, Rousdon. Roger was very impressed with the way that she handled the job and invited her to become Lady Warden at Lee Abbey, but she did not accept. After having served in the army during the war, and then being involved in relief work in Germany, she did not feel at all keen about the idea of living in a Community . However, Roger was not the sort of person to take 'no' for an answer. A year and a half later he was still asking her to come as Lady Warden. In the end she agreed to come for six months, until they could find somebody else. She was to stay for twenty-eight years!

Yet another important arrival along with Madeleine and Jack in the spring of 1948 was a herd of nine cows. In fact eight had been expected, but one had calved on the way! They formed the nucleus of the Lee Abbey farm which still has an important place in the work of the Community. Their purchase marked a significant policy decision for the Council. After careful consideration they had decided that it would be right to farm the estate commercially. It was a brave step, for it involved taking out a further loan of £3,000 on top of the loans already outstanding on the original purchase of the building.

In the same way as Nehemiah rebuilt the walls of Jerusalem, or the Lord had called on St. Francis to rebuild the church of San Damiano, the physical work needed to restore the Lee Abbey building and estate was a visual parable of the work of God through the Community in rebuilding His Church. There was much rubbish and debris which had to be cleared away; there were parts that had fallen into disuse which had to be restored to their former purpose; there were areas that needed radical alteration in order to meet current needs, and above all the full potential of all that God had provided needed to be discovered and put to use. The task of Lee Abbey was to encourage the Church to realise the full potential of the resources offered to it by Christ; to discover the power of God to change people's lives and equip them for service. The Church possessed tremendous resources in its membership, which it did not know how to use. Part of the vision of Lee Abbey was to provide the training to discover and develop the ministry of lay people, in a Church where it was too often felt that ministry was the province of the professional clergy.

Together with the building, the Trustees had purchased 350 acres of land. About 190 acres of this was in the form of woodland; a further 60 acres, consisting of the former golf course around the house and Crockpits (the headland beyond Lee Bay) was capable of cultivation. The remaining 100 acres at Caffyns Down, which had formed a second golf course, was an entirely separate unit which was sold off in 1951.

The only part of the estate which had been consistently maintained was the vegetable garden behind the main house, and the walled garden with its two glasshouses. These had provided a valuable supply of fruit and vegetables for the school. With rationing still a major problem, these gardens continued to be an important source of food for Community and guests.

Squire Bailey had laid out the main part of the estate in the last century. Woodland was planted with Sessile oaks, and a network of paths was constructed through the woods and along the coast.

After twenty-five years of neglect the woodlands presented a major problem. An enormous amount of work had to be done to hack through the undergrowth and reclaim the paths, clearing out many of the trees that came down in the gales each year. Then, as now, they provided a more than adequate supply of logs for use in the house, and were even a useful additional source of income. If the character of the woods was to be maintained for future generations, then a large amount of thinning out and replanting was necessary. Even today the Community is still very conscious of the vast amount of work that needs to be done in the woods, if they are to be preserved for the future.

Another obvious way of augmenting the food supply was to keep livestock. Pop looked after a number of chickens and ducks down at Lower Lodge, and there were a couple of pigs. The first two pigs – Gert and Daisy – proved to be a great success and so were succeeded by Bits and Bobs. Stewed rabbit was also a very familiar item on the menu of most of the early houseparties. But although good to eat, the vast number of rabbits on the estate proved a real problem, and when a couple of fields were ploughed up to grow potatoes, cabbages and mangolds, they had to be wired to a depth of nine inches to keep the rabbits out.

The first cows were Welsh Blacks, a very hardy breed that could live off the rough pasture, and stay outside throughout the winter. The farm buildings were very rudimentary, and for milking the cows would be tethered to a row of posts outside and of course milked by hand. If it was raining then you got more milk! Their milk was extremely rich and the guests greatly appreciated the plentiful bowls of clotted cream. It was only as the land improved that these Welsh Blacks were replaced by the Ayrshires which make up the present herd.

All this initial work of clearing the woods and establishing the farm was supervised by the first estate manager, John Ellis, until he left the Community to prepare for ordination. However the work could never have been done without a great deal of outside help, and especially from the student working parties. These have been arranged every year since 1946, and still play a crucial part in maintaining the estate. Three weekly working parties are held during the Easter vacation, and students come and spend part of their time working and the rest sharing in normal houseparty activities. Some medical students from Birmingham, a couple of parish youth clubs, and a group from Exeter University were among those who came in 1947, but particular links developed with Oxford and Cambridge Universities. Both Howard Guinness, the Chaplain of the Oxford pastorate, and Stanley Betts, who worked with the Cambridge pastorate, would bring down groups of students. Both pastorates welcomed the evangelistic ministry of Lee Abbey as complementary to their own work. The clear message of the epilogues, presenting the claims of Christ and the challenge of personal commitment, provided direct teaching without narrowness.

The experience which the working parties offered, of being able to work alongside the Community, and so share more deeply in the life of the place, was to have a profound influence in many lives. They continue to hold an important place in the yearly programme.

# 6

# A Developing Ministry

News of the great things that God was doing in North Devon soon began to spread as guests returned home full of all that they had experienced. Of all those whose lives were changed by Christ at Lee Abbey during those years, probably none was to become better known at the time than Dr. Jim Bell-Nichol. He was a G.P. and became a regular contributor to a very popular radio programme called 'The Silver Lining'.

It was the first week of April in 1947, and a friend had persuaded him, rather reluctantly, to go with his family and stay at Lee Abbey for a much-needed break. He knew a little about the nature of the place, but he was, as he put it, 'prepared to put up with a modicum of religion for the sake of a pleasant environment.' However, each evening he did attend the epilogue, even though there was no compulsion to do so. He described what happened.

> I attended the epilogues. Amongst those who spoke was one I mentally classified as an old boy; not an old, old boy, but a young old boy. In fact I believe he was then rising sixty-four. He took an epilogue on prayer. My own views on prayer were simplicity itself. You asked for a thing. Sometimes you got it, sometimes you didn't. Extremely unreliable, but anyway, if nothing else was on the carpet, it was worth a shot.
>
> I went to bed. You know how it is when you have something very much on your mind. You hear the clock strike one, two and three. There was no clock, so I

discovered the lumps in the mattress instead. I turned from one side to the other – what was really troubling me was a long list of nice, fat juicy sins, sins which I knew would have to be dealt with if I was to think of becoming a Christian according to Christ's standards.

Slowly the dawn broke; the list by this time was truly formidable. Anyway, there could be no possible harm in carrying out the young old boy's advice – an hour's prayer – the early morning – PSALM. I tiptoed down to the Chapel at the unhappy hour of six-thirty for my first experience of real prayer. P for praise. I was full of gratitude to God for so many things that P was easy. What's next? S for surrender. S for surrender. I could not go on. It was a complete blank wall as regards prayer. Either no prayer or S for surrender. I had thought about it in the night but had decided it would be a good thing to carry out at some future date, maybe when I went home, and then I wouldn't have to tell people at the epilogues. Most embarrassing. Meantime S for surrender – I hesitated long. I knew only too well what surrender meant for me. Then quite deliberately I said to God, 'O Lord, I surrender, and if there is anything I have not surrendered, help me to see that and give it to Thee also.'

A clergyman came in and moved about the Chapel making preparations for Holy Communion, a service which had entirely slipped my memory when I went there. One reads of a strange peace coming over people at such times; a calm which steals over them. There was no peace, no calm, as far as I was concerned. I stumbled out to the open air, to the beautiful fresh morning of the country. There was only one coherent thought in my head: 'You've done it now, you've probably smoked your last cigarette.' And so I found myself on the way to Jenny's Leap.[1]

[1] J. T. Bell-Nicholl, *The Span of Time: The autobiography of a doctor* (Hodder & Stoughton 1952)

As an eighteen-year-old soldier, in the First World War, Dr. Jim suffered shock, and subsequently had developed agoraphobia – a fear of open spaces. He was terrified of being left alone and if he was any further than 300 yards from another human being, sheer panic would set in. After twenty-nine years he was used to taking the elaborate precautions necessary to avoid such situations, and managed to conceal it from his friends and even his family. Now he was walking out to Jenny's Leap. In his autobiography, *The Span of Time*, he describes what happened next.

And so I found myself on my way to the sea at seven o'clock on an April morning. I must have gone some way before I realised what I was doing. I nearly turned back, but I said to myself – or was it the voice of God speaking to me in my own mind? Go on. I went on. It wasn't very far to the edge of the cliff, just a before-breakfast stroll, but all the same it was further than my agoraphobia would take me. I had got half-way there when my ghost laid his clammy fingers on me. My heart felt as though its thudding would burst through my chest; my breathing became a rapid series of gasps; my mouth became dry. Sheer panic. I stopped in my tracks. Out of the depths of my soul I prayed, as I had prayed so often before, 'God, take this thing away from me.' I can best describe what happened next by saying it was as though I had taken off a heavy overcoat on a summer's day. In a few moments my heart stopped thumping – my breathing became natural – my mouth became moist. I was a free man. I knew in an instant that the spectre had vanished. I remember singing at the top of my voice as I completed my journey to the sea. On my way back I met the Warden. He must have thought I was off my head. I was still singing. To reassure him I told him the whole story.

Next morning before anyone was up I went away to the loneliest place I could find to see if it was true. The panic did not come back; it has never come back.

Psychological laws? Maybe. But who makes the psychological laws work? I am content to thank God for answering my prayer on that April morning – and to leave it at that.

Two years later, Dr. Jim gave his testimony on a radio service broadcast from Lee Abbey, but he was unable to use his own voice, for he had developed multiple sclerosis, a progressive type of paralysis. Yet this crippling disease in no way caused him to regret that surrender of his life to Christ. In that broadcast, he referred to himself as 'the happiest man in England today'. He found many ways of ministering to people by his broadcasts and his writing. He was a frequent visitor to houseparties, and God gave him a very special ministry to many people before his death in 1954.

It would be a most unusual houseparty – and cause for considerable concern – if the final epilogue on the Friday night did not include a number of people like Dr. Jim who shared with the Community and their fellow guests their new-found faith in Christ. Perhaps even more significant than these testimonies were the letters which came to members of the Community, when guests, with their holiday well in the past, shared their excitement, joys and frustrations as they discovered the reality of the Living Christ in their home situations. Here was the evidence that it was the Lord who was at work and that their commitment was not founded upon a purely emotional response.

God was honouring the faith of the founders and was blessing the work of Lee Abbey. It was not that they had discovered a neat evangelistic technique. There were those who, not having visited Lee Abbey, were suspicious that it was practising evangelism by pressure. It was easy to assume that unsuspecting people were being lured to so-called 'holidays' to be, in fact, subjected to direct aggressive or more subtle psychological pressure to become Christians. A visit to Lee Abbey would quickly establish that this was very far from the truth. Although each house-party always had a programme of sessions, discussions and nightly epilogues, it was made very clear that nothing was compulsory, and, as now, there is no disapproval of those who choose to do other things. The only pressure felt at Lee Abbey is the pressure of the Holy Spirit convicting a person from within; no one is approached with any 'hard-sell' evangelistic strategy. There are many people for whom Lee Abbey is simply a place to enjoy a relaxing holiday in a friendly atmosphere, 'to charge the batteries' for the rest of the year.

It is not possible to analyse neatly the means that God uses to touch people at Lee Abbey. Different guests testify to different things. Yet in the end, the majority comment that it is 'somehow the atmosphere of the whole place'. Many remark that they are struck by this as soon as they arrive. There is something different, but they can't put their finger on it. This can also have an adverse effect. There is a story of one girl from a family with no Christian background, who was coming down to the Youth Camp held each year in August. Her parents brought her down by car, and as they passed through the gateway at the Top Lodge, her father commented upon the atmosphere. By the time they had driven a few hundred yards further on the road to the Entrance Tower, he could stand it no longer. He told his daughter to get out of the car, gave her the luggage and suggested that she walked the rest of the way down the hill. He turned the car round and drove away at top speed.

The sheer beauty of the setting makes a profound effect. 'The heavens declare the glory of God' is a ready response to anyone watching a dramatic sunset over Lee Bay, or admiring the variety of views from Duty Point tower. There are those for whom a walk on their own in the woods will be a time to experience the presence of God, as much as any session or talk.

Many guests are also struck by the friendliness of the people, both fellow guests and Community. If their previous experience of Christians has been either of a formal, cold gathering or of false heartiness, then the natural friendliness of very normal people can be a great surprise. Witnessing the life of the Community, not merely when they are talking about Christianity but going about their daily work, makes a powerful impression, especially on those for whom the Church has been seen as a building rather than as a fellowship of people.

The nightly epilogues and morning sessions also made a great impact on many who came to Lee Abbey in those days. For many guests, it was the first time that they had heard the Christian faith simply explained and related to the needs of the modern world. Here indeed was Good News for those who had previously seen Christianity in terms of the obligation of church attendance and of good works, with no idea of being able to enter into a personal relationship with God. Each week the epilogues would follow the same basic theme looking in turn at man's need, God's answer in Christ, and the power of the Holy Spirit. As well as the talks, epilogues would often include short testimonies from different members of the Community and guests, in which they would share something of how they had come to know Christ, and were experiencing Him at work in their lives. These testimonies, often very nervously given, would speak to people as powerfully as the main talk, for here were ordinary people who demonstrated that it was no theoretical Christ that was being offered.

Whatever means God used to speak to those who came, crucial to all that was going on was the undergirding prayer. There was the daily worship of the Community; the houseparty team, comprising both Community and guests, would meet each day after breakfast to plan and pray for the day's activities; a group of people prayed each night during the epilogue for the speaker and for those who were listening; and there were the prayers of the Lee Abbey Friends, people from all over the country who had committed themselves to pray for the work. If Lee Abbey is in the end about the work of God rather than the work of man, then indeed it is this prayer which is the key to all that happens.

Lee Abbey was probably to have a greater impact on those from overseas than on any other group of people. Since the first houseparty season in 1946 it had been decided that an International Houseparty should be a feature of the programme. Yet these houseparties were far from easy.

Memories of the war were still very fresh in people's minds as the guests gathered for the International Houseparty at the end of August in 1947. The atmosphere was distinctly cold, as many people began to realise exactly who had accepted the invitation to the houseparty. As well as those from England there were groups from France, Holland, Germany and Switzerland. For the Dutch and the French it was the first time since the war that they had met any Germans. On the third evening, during the epilogue one of the Germans stood up and asked if he might speak.

'I was a leader in the Nazi Youth. Now I am a Christian. I ask that you accept my apologies for all that my people did to your people during the war. Please forgive us.'

That apology, not merely the fact that forgiveness had been sought but that it was given, transformed the houseparty. As the fortnight progressed each person began to discover what they thought was impossible, how in Christ their natural hatred and prejudice could be overcome as they shared and worshipped together. At the end of the fortnight a seven-point declaration was produced which was sent to the religious press of the countries involved. It began:

We who have been present at the International Houseparty at Lee Abbey from Holland, France, Germany, Switzerland and England, have experienced in a new way the reality of Jesus Christ as the One through whom alone real unity between nations is possible.

Therefore we are convinced:

1. That faith in Christ as Saviour and Lord alone creates such unity.
2. That by our surrender to Christ, national hatred and pride, prejudice and ill-will have been overcome, and spiritual unity, love and fellowship brought about.
3. That this experience came through the power of the Holy Spirit, the challenge of the Word of God revealed in Christ and united worship and prayer.

There were tears in the eyes of many as on the last day the whole houseparty shared together in a service of Holy Communion held in the brilliant sunshine on the north lawn.

A letter to the Community from a surgeon at Bonn University expressed something of what the Germans felt.

It was such a delightful holiday at Lee Abbey. Not only meeting other nationalities and Christians of other de-nominations but it was more the whole spirit of the place. And it was this spirit which helped to overcome the rather awkward feeling which we Germans have towards other nations, this feeling of guilt and shame which some of us tried to overcome by pride. I want you to know how grateful I am for the opportunity to see and experience again the power of the Living Christ.

The Community had discovered another very important element of the ministry that God had for them: to be a place of reconciliation, where individuals and groups can discover what it means to both forgive and to be forgiven for acts that often go back many years. In more recent times the Lord has brought into being a number of communities for whom this is to be a primary work, such as the community at Rostrevor in Northern Ireland.

Links between Lee Abbey and churches on the continent

continued to grow. Several houseparties and training weeks were organised by Lee Abbey in Holland itself, and close links were established with Corrie Ten Boom. Following her war-time experience in the Ravensbruck concentration camp, she had a powerful speaking ministry taking her to many countries, especially Germany, testifying to the power of God to overcome bitterness and prejudice. She had been one of the guests at that houseparty in 1947 and included visits to Lee Abbey as part of her busy travelling schedule.

The closeness of the links that developed between Lee Abbey and Holland resulted in the visit of Princess Wilhelmina to a houseparty in 1951. During the war she had been Queen of the Netherlands but had abdicated in favour of her daughter. Not even in the days of old Squire Bailey had Lynton seen anything quite like this!

A Dutch pastor had indicated that if the Community were to invite the Princess to visit, she would probably accept, as she was very interested in all she had heard about Lee Abbey. The invitation was sent, but apart from a formal acknowledgement from her secretary, nothing further was heard. Then quite unexpectedly came the news that she was planning to come for a week in September! The house was already fully booked and was not really furnished for royalty, but she decided that she would stay at the Tors Hotel in Lynmouth and come out each day to Lee Abbey. The local taxi, 'Bod', was pressed into service, and each day with the driver in peaked cap and white gloves, the Princess and her lady-in-waiting drove through Lynton to Lee Abbey. On the final day of the houseparty she attended the Communion service in the big lounge, to receive Holy Communion in the Anglican Church for the first time. At the final epilogue she asked if she might speak:

'I will not forget what I have learned in your Community. I was glad to experience the spirit of brotherhood and understanding among us all. It is wonderful to see how all differences, everything vanishes before the Living Christ and our unity in Him becomes real, a unity manifested in having intercommunion.

'When we go back to our duties and our homes, let us tell all who are willing to work for Christ, to make sure that what they are planning for, or have planned, fits in with His plan, for rescuing mankind out of the entanglement of today.

'May Christians all over the world (and all who are of goodwill help them too) join in and partake of His activity, where they see Him at work in all expressions of life, and make Christianity a concrete reality, and for everyone practically acceptable, by giving great opportunities of serving God and our fellow men.

'May, just as we have formed unity during this meeting at Lee Abbey, the Churches all over the world, seek and find evermore *their* Unity in Christ, and so their unity becomes the Apostle of Peace to our world, torn asunder by division and strife.'

A pine tree planted by the Princess in the field in front of the house is a reminder of a very memorable visit by someone who was felt by all to be a very gracious Christian lady.

In these early years Lee Abbey was clearly a place that the Lord was blessing, but few guests realised that behind the scenes things were far from easy. When the auditors were asked to prepare the financial accounts for 1947–8, to be presented to the Council, it became clear that there was a considerable administrative confusion. It was necessary to distinguish between the work of Lee Abbey for which the Council was responsible, and other ventures under the name of Pathfinder such as external houseparties and publishing. Roger was anxious to push forward and implement his ideas, while the Council was increasingly anxious to make sure that Lee Abbey was based on a sound footing. Part of Roger's original vision had been for a training scheme during the winter months. A scheme was proposed and in 1949 a Director of Training had been appointed, but the Council did not feel able to go ahead with the appointment.

If the devil could not frustrate the work from the outside, he was trying to undermine it from within. When a new member is admitted to full membership of the Lee Abbey Community he is asked this question, 'Are you prepared to live in fellowship, being open to be known for what we are, accepting one another in Christ, and saying of others nothing that could not be said to them personally if love and wisdom required it?' This question is included in the Community promises out of the experience that it is in the area of relationships that the Community is most vulnerable. During 1948 and 1949 there had been an increasing breakdown of relationships within the senior Community at Lee Abbey. At the Council meeting on March 10th, 1950 Roger offered his resignation as Warden of Lee Abbey and it was accepted.

# 7

# The Three Musketeers

'You had better send in to me any names that come to you and I will shortlist them,' suggested Geoffrey Rogers, chairman of the Lee Abbey Council; they were discussing the crucial question of the appointment of the new Warden. It was going to take some time to get used to the idea of Lee Abbey without Roger de Pemberton. Indeed there were some people who questioned whether it could survive without his drive and enthusiasm. It was Roger to whom the Lord had given the initial vision and it was he who had gathered round him those who were to implement it. It was essential that his successor should be a person who shared that same vision for evangelism and the renewal of the Church.

It was early on a Monday morning – closing day for sending in the nominations. Geoffrey and Dora were still in bed when Dora suddenly said, 'What if somebody suggests you?' It was the first time that the possibility had occurred to either of them, but now the idea suddenly gripped them. Geoffrey got out of bed and went to kneel beside Dora. Together they prayed that the Lord would guide them and show them His way.

When Geoffrey arrived at his office at C.M.S. Headquarters in Salisbury Square his secretary pointed out five letters, each marked 'Confidential', waiting on his desk. All the letters were brief. Each in turn had only one name to suggest, 'Geoffrey Rogers'.

His appointment was confirmed at the next meeting of

the Council in April. Roger had agreed to remain at Lee Abbey until the end of the summer season and so on Michaelmas Day, September 29th, 1950, Geoffrey was installed as the second Warden of Lee Abbey, a post he was to hold for the next fourteen years.

Geoffrey had been brought up in Cambridge where he went to school and university. During his first term as an undergraduate at St. Catherine's College, he came across the children's evangelist, Hudson Pope. Many years before this same man had been used by God to bring the young Leslie Sutton to faith in Christ. Geoffrey had been asked by his mother to take his younger sisters to a C.S.S.M. meeting in a house just outside the city. He was asked in by the hostess, felt too embarrassed to refuse and so heard the Gospel explained and began to wonder about its relevance to his life. His curiosity aroused, he went to further meetings until he committed his life to Christ.

There was plenty to encourage a young Christian to grow in Cambridge, and it was not long before he began to sense that God was calling him to the ordained ministry. After taking his degree he went to theological college at Ridley Hall to prepare for ordination. Not having moved from Cambridge he was able to keep close links with many of his university friends and was introduced to Dora Howden, a young undergraduate from Girton College with whom he promptly fell in love.

On being ordained deacon in 1927 he went as assistant curate to St. James', Gravesend, while Dora remained in Cambridge to complete her degree. At that time, the main evangelical Christian society in Cambridge (the C.I.C.C.U.) was a strictly male preserve and the women's equivalent was C.W.I.C.C.U. – the Cambridge Women's Inter-College Christian Union – of which Dora was student President. One weekend she was entertaining a guest speaker, Bishop Linton of Iran (then called Persia). A photograph of Geoffrey on Dora's mantelpiece reminded the Bishop of the young man whom he had met at a

C.S.S.M. meeting five years previously. He enquired for news of Geoffrey and as a result, after only two years at Gravesend, Geoffrey went out as a missionary to Iran with C.M.S. Dora joined him two years later and they were married in Isfahan. As well as being the Bishop's Chaplain, Geoffrey was pastor of the Church in Isfahan and chaplain to the British Community in Teheran. By 1939 they were due to come home on furlough. They arrived back in England in February but the outbreak of war made it impossible for them to return. With their future very uncertain, C.M.S. appointed Geoffrey to their Headquarters Staff and he became Candidates Secretary. Like all missionaries he was expected to do his share of deputation work – speaking in parishes about the work of the Society and the needs of the Church overseas. It was this that took him, in July 1943, to speak at the annual missionary meeting in Cuthbert Bardsley's parish in Woolwich. Cuthbert was very impressed by Geoffrey's concern for evangelism and invited him to take part in a Holy Week Mission the following year. Another member of that mission team was Jack Winslow, so for the first time Geoffrey heard of Lee Abbey and about the plan to purchase the building in Devon. Geoffrey already knew Roger de Pemberton; they had been contemporaries at Cambridge. He was excited by the vision for evangelism that the Lee Abbey project offered and so, with his experience in Iran and his connections with C.M.S. Headquarters he was an obvious person to become one of the seven Trustees.

A new phase in the story of Lee Abbey began with Geoffrey's arrival as Warden in September 1950. The traumas of the early years were to be followed by a long period of stability, in which all that had been pioneered was set on a firmer footing and consolidated. God had brought together three men to lead the second stage of Lee Abbey's ministry.

Geoffrey, Leslie and Jack came to be known as the 'Three Musketeers' as they led the Community over the next ten years. It was an unlikely trio: they were very different in temperament, background and age. Each had first-hand missionary experience but they came from very different spiritual positions, although they shared a common passion for evangelism. Together they formed a powerful team.

Geoffrey, as Warden, was very much the leader, although the youngest of the three – ten years junior to Leslie and twenty years to Jack. Full of energy, it seemed he could turn his hand to anything. He took a keen practical interest in the working of the estate; he found great delight in driving a tractor during the student working parties, and he would always go to bed with his wellingtons and torch nearby should one of the diesel generators need attention in the night. An enthusiastic pianist and singer, he would take responsibility for the training of the choir for the tableau on Christmas Eve each year, auditioning every new, highly nervous Community member!

There were some of his friends who felt that by coming to Lee Abbey, with stoles, candles and links with Anglo-Catholics, Geoffrey must have abandoned his conservative evangelical position. This was still a time when evangelicals in the Church of England tended to be defensive of their position and were highly suspicious of other traditions or any possible suggestion of 'compromising their message'. Yet anyone who heard Geoffrey speak could have no doubt of his evangelical convictions, with his clear, simple presentation of the Gospel and his stress on the need for personal conversion by repentance and commitment to Christ. Lee Abbey stressed 'Christmanship' rather than 'churchmanship' and Geoffrey wholeheartedly welcomed this approach. As time progressed the experience of working with people like Jack enabled him to appreciate and value other traditions, though for a long time some people felt that he was rather cautious about the Catholic and the sacramental.

Leslie Sutton was every bit as warm-hearted as Geoffrey,

yet his role in the Community was very different. He was still suffering the effects of his wounding at Gallipoli; severe headaches were a recurring problem and at times this meant that he was not always easy to work with. His stammer meant that he could be almost inarticulate yet the message got across as he hammered away at the great truths he had learned: the need for adventurous faith in God and to experience the power of the Holy Spirit.

Leslie had almost the manner of an Old Testament prophet as he thundered his message, and it was in his exposition of books like Jeremiah and Ezekiel that he was most powerful. For some, his very direct evangelistic technique was rather overpowering, as he would quite literally collar someone, grasping them by the shoulder. Yet this was the approach which God used to reach those who would have avoided any less direct challenge. As the layman of the three his contribution at Lee Abbey demonstrated to clergy and laity alike that spiritual ministry is not the sole preserve of the ordained clergy.

The third member of the triumvirate, Jack Winslow, was different again. His presence ensured that Lee Abbey could not be labelled simply 'evangelical'. He brought with him a wealth of spirituality from his Anglo-Catholic background and time in India. His age and style of life meant that he was the father confessor figure in the Community in both the formal and informal sense. His daily quiet time – an unhurried time of prayer and reflection at the beginning of the day – was of prime importance to Jack, both in his teaching and in his personal life. Nobody was quite sure what time he got up each day, but it must have been around five-thirty a.m. Yet early rising also meant an early bedtime and at ten o'clock whatever else might be happening, Jack would make it quite clear that the time had arrived for him to retire to bed.

While he was an undergraduate at Oxford Jack had heard the American evangelist, John R. Mott, speaking about 'the morning watch' and so began a practice that he was to continue for the rest of his life. Writing in his book *When I Awake* he says,

> I can now confidently say, if in these years I have been able to accomplish any useful service to God or man, I owe it to no other single cause so much as to the habit then started of keeping the morning watch. My experience over these years has taught me that this quiet hour spent with God day by day is an unfailing secret of power, progress, purpose and peace.[1]

The way he spent this quiet time evolved over the years. His reading of Christian mystics, like Lady Julian of Norwich, together with his experience of Indian mysticism, brought new dimensions to his prayer and Bible reading. The Oxford Group had added a further strand. Its teaching laid great stress on the need to spend a time each day waiting on God to receive divine guidance about every decision of daily life. This was seen as coming both through the reading of the Scriptures and also, with one's mind concentrated on God, waiting for direction. In later years the Oxford Group was to receive justified criticism of this practice which could cause people to misinterpret their own whims as being the guidance of God, sometimes with distressing consequences. Yet for Jack this waiting upon God was rooted in his prayer life and study of the Bible, and became a source of daily strength in living a life which was each day surrendered to God.

Although Jack was the person at Lee Abbey always identified with teaching about the morning quiet time it would be quite wrong to assume that he was alone in his emphasis on its importance. Both Geoffrey and Leslie were as insistent both in their teaching and by their own personal example, that anyone who wanted to take the Christian life seriously must spend time alone with God each day. It was expected of the Community; the Community promises

[1] J. C. Winslow, *When I Awake* (thoughts on the keeping of the morning watch), Hodder, 1957.

include the question, 'Have you accepted the discipline of regular private collection through Bible reading and daily prayer?' Although this question does not specify the early morning, it was generally understood that this was the best time. Four things were considered essential for the young Christian at Lee Abbey – a Bible, a notepad, a pen and an alarm clock! The most compelling feature of Jack's teaching about the quiet time was that his life was evidence of the supreme worth of what he was saying.

As Geoffrey was a musician, Jack was a poet, writing many poems and hymns, including some that have become popular such as 'Lord of all Hopefulness' sung to the popular Irish tune 'Slane', and 'Lord of Lords and King Eternal' both of which have been published in several modern hymn books. He was also an accomplished author, producing a steady stream of popular books, including *The Lee Abbey Story*.

These three men provided the Community with a leadership that was clearly authoritarian but was deeply respected. It would be wrong to assume that relationships were always easy, but the key to their unity was their commitment to team-work – the style of working propounded by the Oxford Group. This was not an easy way to choose. They had to make themselves vulnerable if they were to be fully open with each other. In this way, as they discussed and prayed together, a deep trust developed. Even when they disagreed, they were able to accept Geoffrey's ultimate decision as Warden.

They were three great men of faith and the task which they undertook required no less faith than had the initial establishment of Lee Abbey. Indeed in some ways it required more, as they began to explore ways of recognising and developing the full potential of the work.

The Community itself offered great possibilities: here was the greatest resource for evangelism that Lee Abbey had been given. The deeper the commitment of the Community to Christ and to each other, the more effective would be its witness. However, it was not easy to establish and maintain a depth of commitment when the membership of the Community was constantly changing and it was known that many people's involvement was only for a limited time. The recruitment of suitably mature Christians willing to stay for some time was clearly essential. Even more crucial was the need to set up a Community structure which would encourage Christian growth. To this end the significance of red and green badges, denoting full and probationary members, was altered. It was decided that Community promises should be made in two stages. After one month at Lee Abbey people became associate members, volunteering 'a sincere desire to learn and walk in the way of Christ', 'loyalty to the aims and work of Lee Abbey', 'willingness to accept the challenge of the place of private prayer and Bible study', and to attend Community prayers and the weekly associates' meeting. After six months they could ask to be received into full membership, assenting to a series of searching promises:

> full commitment to Christ: a surrender which is real, practical, involving the stewardship of our talents, our minds, our time, our possessions and all our relationships . . .
> Co-operation in building up the fellowship of the Spirit in the Community with complete honesty and love toward one another, our willingness to be known for what we are without pose or unreality, to take and give constructively, to say concerning others only what we would be prepared to say to them personally if love and wisdom required it, and to be 'girded with humility to serve one another' . . .
> Determination to make our work part of our witness and to be satisfied with nothing less than the best for Christ's sake and an eagerness to undertake personal evangelism.

The same basic principles of membership still apply, although periodic reviews have simplified the wording and caused less differentiation between short- and long-term members. At the time of writing there is one set of Community promises which can be made after a person has been at Lee Abbey for three months.

Changes to deepen the commitment of the Community included the introduction of a system of allowances. Initially certain members of Community had been paid a salary, although when money was very short many of them had been willing to forego pay completely. It was agreed that all Community members, irrespective of their jobs, should be paid the same small allowance in addition to receiving their board and lodging. A scale of increments according to length of service is now provided, but the principle is that people are paid according to their need rather than as a reward for service. As the majority of Community members stay at Lee Abbey for only a limited time, it has always been important for members to maintain some financial independence, and so no common pooling of money has ever been considered.

With the deepening of the discipleship of the Community came the development of the Friends – 'the Community writ large' as they have been called. The fellowship of Lee Abbey Friends was established almost from the beginning. It had a two-fold purpose; to encourage the prayer support and financial backing that was essential for the maintenance of the work and also to provide follow-up support and encouragement to those who had been to houseparties.

Here was another great potential to be realised, not only for Lee Abbey but as a spiritual fighting force throughout the country. To try to dispel the image that a Friend was someone who supported a building, rather like the friends of some ancient church or cathedral, the title was changed from Friends of Lee Abbey to Lee Abbey Friends of Jesus. A simple admission service was introduced during the final evensong of each houseparty, and Friends were asked to renew this commitment each year. It stated that Friends were those who: 'have committed themselves personally to Christ the Saviour and Lord; are prepared to work through prayer and witness for the conversion of others; pray regularly for the renewal of the Church, for the work of Lee Abbey and for the other Friends'.

To enable Friends in a particular area to contact each other a geographical list was introduced. This was a tricky area for Lee Abbey and continues to be so. A real danger that faces any Christian centre like Lee Abbey is that people will see it as an alternative to their local church. The stated purpose of the Community has always been that it exists to support local churches. Guests at Lee Abbey are constantly encouraged to be fully involved with and committed to their local congregation however difficult and discouraging it may be. It would be a complete contradiction of this if Lee Abbey were then to start organising events in various places, independent of the local churches.

In practice, however, there have always been some people whose lives have been touched by God at Lee Abbey, but who have not found any encouragement or opportunities for service when they returned home. They have needed the support of other Lee Abbey Friends in prayer and in helping them to find a suitable church. Often it has been Lee Abbey alone that has continued to challenge them to stand and act for God. As numbers increased, from less than 1,000 in 1950 to nearly 7,000 by the end of the decade, the Friends became very important to the work of Lee Abbey. Many local churches were blessed through the ministry of Christians who were receiving support and encouragement as Lee Abbey Friends. There could have been a danger of the Friends acting as little more than an 'old boys' club' useful for raising money; in fact they had become a significant witness for Christ throughout the country.

Paul, a member of the senior management of a large company, was a Lee Abbey Friend who came to value this fellowship very much. He had become a Christian in middle age when at the height of his career. Although he had been brought up as a member of the Church of England, had been baptised and confirmed and attended school chapel, religion meant absolutely nothing to him. Money and success were his motives. As he wrote of himself,

> I was worldly, living a life in which ambition had me by the throat and was the main driving force in my life: a life in which money meant power, and money and success were seen as the ultimate satisfaction for the restlessness which consumed me. The awful jockeying for promotion; the perpetual fear of being beaten to the coveted position; the bitterness, the jealousy resulting in sleepless nights, seemed to be the natural order of things.

As his children grew up, a feeling that he should let them know there was a thing called 'religion' prompted him to start taking them to church.

> I do not know if something in a service, prayers or sermon, now forgotton, touched off a spark somewhere deep inside me but sitting one day on the terrace of a seaside hotel, when on holiday, I felt a sudden burning desire to know more, coupled with a sudden realisation that God was real and what was more, was real to me. At that moment I know now that in His mercy He touched me on the shoulder.

Some weeks later on Maundy Thursday, much to the horror of Dawn, his wife, he slipped away from an important business cocktail party to attend a service in a village church. While talking to the vicar after this service he heard about Lee Abbey and at his suggestion booked to attend one of the Lee Abbey training weekends at Swanwick.

As soon as he arrived at the weekend, very much the businessman with his smart car and immaculate suit, the

Team spotted that here was a man in need. Paul felt distinctly ill at ease in this different environment and tried to keep himself in the background. It was Leslie who managed to take him aside and talk with him, explaining to him for the first time the possibility of a personal relationship with Christ. Within a few minutes Paul was on his knees committing his life to Christ. Later he wrote, 'That surrender and committal did not come quickly or easily, nor is it completed yet. There seems to be a recurring period when one seems to have really advanced, and then the miserable ego pops up and one seems to be back to square one again.' Becoming a Christian was to have drastic consequences for Paul and his family.

People soon began to notice a difference. Dawn, who did not immediately share Paul's new-found faith, felt acutely embarrassed as he would start talking about God at dinner parties, and many of their friends began to drift away, confused about what was happening to them. The family also noticed his changed attitude towards them; they were no longer merely appendages to his career, but they were being loved in a new way, as children of God. The whole quality of their family life was being transformed.

Regular visits to Lee Abbey first as guests and then as speakers became an important part of their life. The Community could witness their Christian growth. One day a gold cigarette lighter was found on the table in Chapel. There was no doubt where it had come from or that another step forward had been made.

At first they found no support from their local church. It seemed to them that their vicar had lost his faith and he looked askance at a suggestion that he might join them in a Bible study group in their home. It was now that the Friends were so valuable, for they were linked with other Lee Abbey people in their area and joined a prayer group. They came to value enormously the mutual support that the Friends provided.

Seven years after Paul and Dawn had become Christians,

Paul's job became increasingly full of tension. He seemed to make no headway in witnessing to his fellow businessmen, and on the Board of Directors he was constantly finding himself at odds with his colleagues. Eventually the day came when he felt unable to consent to a proposal involving making a number of workers redundant. He was in a minority of one. It was suggested to him that if he really could not agree then he should reconsider his position as a member of the Board; he offered his resignation. He felt that his colleagues could not understand his attitude, but his stand must have had some effect because in the end no jobs were lost.

Paul, however, now had no job, three children at school, a large house and all the burdens of a top-level businessman. He was over fifty years of age, but in a strange way confidence replaced anxiety. 'I find it hard to describe the succeeding months, a time of joy when without the continuous presence of Christ there would be despair, when as a family we all drew closer together, where the strains of the situation could have aroused recrimination and apartness.' It was nine months before Paul got a suitable job. In the meantime the family had to live on their capital. It was a great test of their faith and it was only when they no longer had sufficient money for the following month that a job appeared.

For the Community, Paul's experience brought encouragement and a renewed sense of responsibility in their work, as it demonstrated the consequences of following Christ.

And Lee Abbey Friends, no less than the Community, knew that they were being called by God to live out the life of faith.

# 8

## *The God Who Provides*

'Where God guides, He also provides' is a familiar saying, and in retrospect the history of Lee Abbey is a powerful testimony to its truth. Yet the fact that God really is faithful in keeping His promises is often discovered slowly and painfully, and only with the realisation that faith is itself a gift of the Holy Spirit. God has promised to provide what we need rather than what we desire. If we ask, we will receive, though it may not be either in the way or with the timing that we had assumed. One reason is that God's vision is often so much grander than man's. Few of those involved in the founding of Lee Abbey in the 1940s would have imagined that it could have grown to the size and position that it has in the 1980s.

The history of Lee Abbey is rich in incidents where God has dramatically and spectacularly demonstrated His power. Such stories strengthen us, perhaps coming as a rebuke to our lack of faith by reminding us that God really does answer prayer. However one cannot pretend that there are not also stories of disappointment where a prayer, offered in faith, has not been answered in the way that was confidently expected. Such disappointments are often only to be tempered in the light of future events when God's true purposes are seen.

God's greatest provision at Lee Abbey is people. Time after time God has called just the right people to fill vacant places on the Community. Experience shows that God does know Lee Abbey's needs. Yet there have been times when manpower has seemed lacking, and God's word to the Community has been to discover within the existing members previously unrecognised talents, be it for cooking, milking cows or counselling somebody in deep distress.

God's hand has been seen continually in the financial provision for the work. Lee Abbey was managed on a shoestring, and financial needs were not kept a secret – indeed the shortage of money was apparent to any who came to stay. It was not unknown for the payment of Community allowances to depend on the receipts from the toll road. Often urgent needs have been met through gifts of money or goods from guests.

One typical situation was faced by the Community in 1948. The previous summer had seen fewer guests than planned, and was followed by a winter period during which the Community received virtually no income. By June nearly £2,000 was owing to tradesmen in the Lynton area. Leslie had witnessed similar situations before, in the W.E.C., and he felt very strongly that this should not be allowed to continue: it was dishonouring to God. He was determined that by the end of the month God wanted these debts to be cleared, and so the money must be prayed for. Specific prayer was offered that the Lord would provide £2,000 by the end of the month. Leslie added a postscript to his prayer. 'Lord, may it come in large sums, so that we don't have to write too many receipts!' Midway through the month a piece of paper was pushed into Leslie's breast pocket as he stood talking to a guest in the octagonal lounge. Absent-mindedly he pushed his spectacles on top of it and did not find it until the next morning. It was a cheque for £1,000. Those in the Community, who were aware of the situation, thanked God for this cheque and confidently waited for Him to provide the other £1,000. Yet it was not until the very last day, on June 30th, that another cheque was received, again for £1,000. The prayer had indeed been answered, and only two receipts were written!

Yet at the same time as this most direct answer to prayer

there was a great disappointment. In May Lee Abbey had undertaken its biggest publicity exercise yet. A glossy brochure entitled *Counter Attack* had been produced. It set out in stirring language the vision for evangelism in Britain that lay behind the work of Lee Abbey.

> We believe and expect great response in prayer, interest, gifts of money and legacies, and full co-operation in making the work and its needs widely known. Will you stand together with us in faith and prayer – regular prayer that all God's purposes for this work may be fulfilled; will you get quiet with God and see if He wants you to give in any way to this work? We ask only for that help which you believe is guided of God.

Yet God apparently did not guide. Fifteen thousand copies were sent out to both clergy and laity, yet the only visible response was a handful of encouraging letters and about £120. It was a monumental flop, and an expensive one, at a time when Lee Abbey could not afford it. The prayers of the Friends had been sought through the newsletter to back this distribution, but God had clearly shown that financial needs were not to be met in this way.

However, the Lord was not allowing Lee Abbey to run at a deficit. Each year the giving of the Lee Abbey Friends and other donations meant that the accounts could show a small excess of income over expenditure. At the same time a large sum had to be paid against the mortgage, which had hardly been reduced at all in the first five years. In 1950 there was still over £25,000 outstanding, costing nearly £1,000 a year in interest. An appeal was made through the newsletter for offers of interest-free and low-interest loans in order to pay off the mortgage to the bank and so avoid these high costs. Sufficient offers of loans came in, and so a debenture issue was made possible. An unexpected source of income came when it was discovered that Caffyns Down

(100 acres of unused land) could be sold for three times its estimated value!

From 1952, each year saw a significant reduction in the outstanding debt of £20,000. By 1955 only £2,545 remained to be paid off. That year marked the tenth anniversary of the founding of Lee Abbey and it was decided to mark the occasion by moving the annual London reunion service, normally held in St. Martin-in-the-Fields, to St. Paul's Cathedral. To some it seemed a very ambitious vision but over 3,000 Lee Abbey Friends and guests packed the cathedral for the great service of thanksgiving. The day was to be a landmark in the history of God's provision for Lee Abbey. It had been decided that the collection at St. Paul's should go towards the clearing of the debt.

In preparation for the service Geoffrey explained to the head verger that a large collection of over £1,000 was anticipated. 'Sir, a collection in four figures would be a record for St. Paul's Cathedral.' Geoffrey's warning was not heeded, for the collection plates and alms dish proved totally inadequate for the amount of money, with pound notes spilling over onto the floor.

The established pattern for the reunion day was that after the Thanksgiving Service during the first part of the afternoon, everybody would move to the Central Hall, Westminster to renew friendships over tea and join in the more informal rally. The rally was well in progress when a telephone call came through from St. Paul's to say that the collection was £2,055. Only £490 remained to clear the debt. Cuthbert Bardsley, the chairman of the Council, put the challenge to the assembled Friends. A time of quiet was kept, and then the collection bags were passed round. Later he announced the total. It was £1,153. Everybody stood and sang: 'Praise God from whom all blessings flow!'

In ten years over £40,000 had been given for the establishment of Lee Abbey. The next year saw another repercussion from that day, when a conference for vergers was held at Lee Abbey!

However, the provision of money is not the only way that God chooses to show His care for His people. From the beginning it was obvious that a chapel would be essential at Lee Abbey, to provide both a room for services, and also a place of quiet for Community and guests. There was not really much choice about where it should be. After the octagonal lounge and the dining room, the next largest room in the house was one on the first floor that had originally been Squire Bailey's bedroom. It was a beautiful light room with a magnificent view over the estate, and dominated by an enormous mirror. The one drawback was that it could seat only about forty people in comfort. This meant that two services of Holy Communion were held each Sunday morning and still many guests would find themselves sitting out on the landing trying to join in the service through the open door. The situation was not helped by the fact that the room was adjacent to a whole line of bathrooms and toilets with their customary noises!

The only option was to build, and in 1951 the Council took the decision to build a new chapel on the North Lawn. It was to be built of local stone, and would cost £5,000. At this time there was still a large amount of money to be repaid on the debt, but it was felt that Friends would readily respond to the appeal.

But God had other ideas about how this need was to be met. After the war the extreme shortage of building materials meant that a licence was necessary for the construction of any new church buildings. The money for the project was beginning to come in, but it became clear that Lee Abbey would not be granted a permit for the project. The only possibility for a new chapel would be if some modification could take place within the existing building.

A new estate manager, Geoffrey Hutchison, had just been appointed and as he walked around the buildings with Geoffrey Rogers an idea came to them. They noticed that on the north side of the house between the two main chimney stacks were three bedrooms. Closer investigation confirmed that these rooms were merely divided by partition walls which had no structural significance. The walls and the ceilings could be removed, and the three bedrooms, together with the passageway, would create one large room with windows on both sides; the ceiling would run up church-fashion into the roof, and it would be capable of seating about 100 people. What is more, one room was on a slightly different level from the other two, which meant that there was already an inbuilt chancel step in exactly the right place!

Once the necessary permission had been granted it took only a matter of days for a very enthusiastic group of students to do the necessary demolition work – throwing the rubble out of the windows onto the north lawn – and to disconnect the old iron radiators and central heating pipes. A local builder did the plastering and Leslie worked on the carpentry with the Community. A few weeks later, at seven a.m. on Easter Day, Geoffrey celebrated Holy Communion in the new chapel for the first time. In a fraction of the time and at virtually no cost God had provided Lee Abbey with a new chapel.

It is so often in this way that God chooses to meet the needs of His people. What we assume can only be achieved by much work and at great expense, is often already ours if only we will recognise it and use it. Many congregations too are often far more conscious of what God has not given them, rather than aware of what He has already provided. The plans for the new building were not abandoned, but set aside, as it was not impossible that God might one day call Lee Abbey to go ahead with this major building project. Nearly thirty years later the idea is still around. In 1981 there was a suggestion that it might be right to proceed with this scheme – now seen as a large meeting room with conference facilities as well as a chapel – but again it was realised that existing buildings could be modified at a fraction of the cost. Work has begun to construct a new meeting room in the back courtyard out of the former table-tennis room.

Other new building has taken place over the years. Desperately needed single rooms were provided in 1955 with the building of twelve single annexes at the back of the main house. In 1957 Garden Lodge was built to provide accommodation for the Warden and his family, separate from the main building. A pair of semi-detached houses, Upper and Lower Close, were constructed in the walled garden in 1959 as more families with young children were joining the Community. The twenty-first anniversary was marked in 1967 with a further building project. This included a new service road at the back of the house, so that goods vehicles no longer had to drive round the front of the house to reach the yard, and a new bedroom block with twelve single guest rooms, a playroom and laundry for guests. Another long cherished vision came to fruition in 1974 when the new kitchen, constructed in the inner courtyard, was completed. This work was done mainly by Community members with a small band of local workmen, and so was completed at about half the estimated contract price. The new kitchen enabled the dining room to be enlarged, and the canteen area to be constructed.

Special gifts came in for all these projects, yet in many ways they were part of the natural development of Lee Abbey. Living conditions for guests and Community alike were improved, in line with the general improvement in living standards throughout the country in the fifties and sixties.

The Community had come to accept with humble gratitude that it was not unusual for a guest to want to make a gift to Lee Abbey, to thank God for what he had received. In 1967 it became known that someone wanted to make a substantial gift: his one condition was that he should remain anonymous. (He came to be referred to affectionately as 'Ben', for benefactor.) It was generally believed that the gift was in thanksgiving to God for the conversion to Christ of two of his children at the Youth Camp. The form of the gift was not to offer a specific sum, but to make money available for any project that would make Lee Abbey more self-sufficient, by improving the facilities of the estate like food production, the water supply and storage of fuel. It was to be up to Lee Abbey to suggest how this might be done and to submit proposals to him.

For many years Ursula had been running the farm in antiquated buildings next to the 'horseboxes' – the annexe occupied by the single men on the Community. Things had, at least, improved since the days when Edna would help milk the cows by hand, tethered to posts outside. The cowshed had been enlarged several times, but still there was only room for twenty cows which were milked by a vacuum bucket system. The milk then had to be carried next door to the dairy to be put into churns. In 1966 Lee Abbey had applied for an improvement grant for the farm buildings. A representative of the Ministry of Agriculture visited and reported that they would not be willing to make a grant for the building on the existing restricted site, but would be prepared to make money available for an entirely new building on a new site. With so many other financial commitments, it seemed very unlikely that Lee Abbey would be able to embark on such an ambitious proposal. Suddenly with the offer from 'Ben' it looked as if this dream might indeed come true.

This was exactly the sort of project that 'Ben' had in mind. A new building would mean that it would be possible to enlarge the herd, provide modern milking machinery and generally increase the efficiency of the whole farm. John Burkett, the architect who had designed the new bedroom block, was asked to draw up plans which were submitted both to the Ministry of Agriculture and also to 'Ben'.

The new farm was built on the site of the old guest car park and came into use in the autumn of 1969. The herd was now almost doubled in size and the cows could be much more efficiently milked and fed. In addition to the actual building, 'Ben's' gift also included new farm and garden implements, a new guest car park and new oil storage tanks. The total value of the gift to Lee Abbey was nearly £18,000.

The farm was to bring publicity to Lee Abbey in an unexpected way. John Burkett had submitted his design for the buildings for a number of awards, and it received three awards, including the Financial Times Industrial Architecture Award for 1970 and a Civic Trust Award. Because Lee Abbey is situated in a National Park, John Burkett had been presented with a difficult task, to design a building which would stand on sloping ground, be functional and also blend in with its environment. The awards indicate that he had indeed succeeded.

No description of the ways in which God has provided and still provides for the needs of Lee Abbey would be complete without something about water. Lee Abbey's remote position means that it has always depended on its own water supply from a number of springs in the hillside above the house. This water is exceptionally pure, and beautiful to drink, but on several occasions, when faced with the very real possibility that the supply might fail, Lee Abbey has been reminded that it is not to be taken for granted. In the early years Lee Abbey also relied on this water supply to generate its electricity.

Nearly every summer Lee Abbey would face the same problem. By August, when the house was at its busiest with the holiday fortnights and the Youth Camp, the number of those living on the estate would be almost doubled, and the level of the water tank would fall dangerously low. Guests became accustomed to the ban on baths and the red ribbons that Madeleine tied onto cistern handles as a reminder that they should only be flushed if absolutely necessary! For Lee Abbey water was a precious gift from God.

Twice a water diviner had been called in. On both occasions water was detected but it was a very long way down, and digging and blasting failed to get through the solid rock through which it could be reached. This was not to be God's solution to the problem.

The water situation reached a crisis point at the end of the long dry summer of 1972. It had now become vital to the running of the house for the water supply to be increased. As the Community prayed it was almost reminiscent of the Children of Israel in the Wilderness crying out to the Lord for water and complaining 'Is the Lord with us or not?'

At this time there was a party of students from Ewell Technical College staying in the house, and they were helping Jack Usher, the engineer, to move some of the plastic water piping higher up the hillside. It was while they were doing this that one of them slipped and dislodged a stone at the side of one of the streams. They noticed that the ground was quite muddy. The next day as Jack dug around the area a new spring, strong and clear, came bubbling out of the bank. It did not take long to get the water tested, and within twenty-four hours of its being connected to the main supply, the water tanks were again filled to overflowing. 'Usher's gusher', as it came to be called, supplied all the water needs of Lee Abbey throughout the seventies, so that even in the very dry summer of 1976 there was no shortage at all. The Sisters of Mary from Darmstadt in Germany gave Lee Abbey a number of slate plaques to be positioned on the estate. One of them was to go above this spring. It reads:

> O sing to the Lord a new song,
> For He has done marvellous things!
> His right hand and His Holy arm
> Have gotten Him the victory.

This spring later failed, and in 1979 it was necessary to look for new sources. Water is now piped from the neighbouring Six Acre Farm, and this availability day by day of fresh running water is the most powerful reminder of God's continual provision for the needs of His people.

# 9

## *The God Who Protects*

With its dramatic coastline and rolling moorland covered with heather, Exmoor must be one of the most beautiful places in England. How good of God to choose such a lovely setting in which to place Lee Abbey. Yet, when the wind howls across the moor and lashes the sea against the rocks, or when the mist descends, Exmoor can quickly become one of the most desolate and wild places in this country. Anyone who lives in Lynton or Lynmouth will know that the weather is not a force to be trifled with, but a power very much in the hands of God.

As so often seems to happen in August, the weather for the first holiday fortnight in 1952 had been very dismal. It seemed to have been raining nearly the whole time and the last day, Friday, August 15th, was certainly no exception. In fact the rain was coming down even harder. In the house it was a matter of keeping the children occupied indoors and doing the packing, but down at the Youth Camp life was not so easy. Many of the tents were leaking and much of the ground in the sleeping area was underwater. If the strong winds continued, much of the night would have to be spent holding the tents down. So after a hurried supper it was decided that the girls should go and sleep that night in the café on the beach, and all the boys should be moved into the big marquee which was on slightly higher ground.

Elsie Savill, the accountant on the Community, also acted as the quartermaster of the camp. Together with David Cole, another member of the Community, she had gone up to the main house to get some dry bedding and make things as comfortable as possible for the girls sleeping on the floor of the beach café. With the girls safely transferred, the Camp Commandant, Raymond Scantlebury, had informal prayers with them and then returned up the road to the main camp field.

By this time, Elsie's tent had begun to leak and she decided that she would go and sleep in her own bed up at the house. The car was parked on the road outside the camp field, and David Cole offered to carry her wet bedding for her. He went on ahead as she laced up the door of her tent.

As soon as David stepped out of the camp field, he found himself swept away by a raging torrent. The road had turned into a fast-flowing river, as the normally gentle stream had burst its bank. It was only by grabbing an old gate post by the Pelton house, fifty yards on, that he was able to stop himself being swept out into the sea. With the tremendous sound of the wind and the rain, Elsie did not hear David's shouts, and as she stepped out of the field she too was swept off her feet, but after being dragged over the stones and rocks for a few yards she was able to get to her feet and clamber out of the water. Struggling to the bank they made their way up to the house to tell Geoffrey what was happening. He telephoned the police who told him that in Lynton they were facing a much greater crisis.

Meanwhile, despite the storm raging outside, the girls at the café had gone to sleep while two members of the team took it in turn to keep watch. About three a.m. they looked out to see that the water was now lapping within an inch and a half of the back door. Together they prayed that the Lord would protect them. They looked out to see that the water was now beginning to subside. It was not until the next morning that they discovered what had happened.

As soon as it was light Geoffrey woke Madeleine and together they went down to the camp. The boys had spent the entire night holding down the tents and they were all safe. Where the road had been, there was now a massive ten-foot hole, and the only way of reaching the girls at the café was to go across the field and scramble down the bank. The girls were all safe – indeed, many of them commented that they had had a very good night's sleep! Not far from the café lay a great tree trunk which had been swept down by the torrent and had been jammed against the sides of the bank. It was probably only this tree that had deflected the course of the new river. If it had not been there, the torrent might have swept straight through the café, almost certainly destroying it and killing many people.

On the Saturday morning, the guests in the house and many of the campers were due to go home. After the events of the previous night it seemed very unlikely that they would be able to get through. A visit to Lynton confirmed that indeed all the roads in the area were blocked, if not washed away. Lynmouth was completely sealed off by the Army, and it was clear that something terrible had happened.

At ten a.m. an Army dispatch rider arrived at Lee Abbey to say that three coaches would be coming in half an hour to pick up all the guests and the campers. One half of the road at Barbrook had been reopened, and the Army was anxious to get all visitors out of the area as quickly as possible. Lynton and Lynmouth faced a severe health hazard, with the drains and mains water supply badly damaged and electricity cut off. Lee Abbey, with its own water and electricity, was virtually the only place in the area functioning normally that day.

Gradually, the full horror of what had happened that night became apparent. Nearly nine inches of rain had fallen on Exmoor in less than twenty-four hours. The moorland streams which fed the East and West Lyn rivers had turned into raging torrents carrying with them a great mass of boulders and torn-up trees. The swollen watercourse swept through Barbrook, and destroyed the entire centre of Lynmouth with its hotels, chapel and harbour. Thirty-four people lost their lives. When Harold Macmillan, then Minister of housing, visited the area, he commented that the scene reminded him of the First World War battlefield at Ypres.

Madeleine tried to see if there were any ways in which the Community could help the flood victims, but it seemed that the W.R.V.S. and the Red Cross had everything well under control and there was little that could be done. On the following Sunday 'Pop' was leading the service at Barbrook Church for which Lee Abbey was responsible at that time. In the congregation as usual was Tom Floyd, a postman from Lynmouth. He had lost six members of his family in the floods, including his wife, one son and one daughter. Tom's faithful dog, Tim, came with him to the service and never let his master out of his sight, even following him around the church as he took the collection.

Apart from damage to the dams, and the loss of the road to the beach, the Lee Abbey estate and all who were staying there that night were completely unharmed by this terrible disaster. A few days after the flood, a national newspaper published an aerial photograph of some tents with a caption describing the makeshift accommodation of the flood victims. It was in fact a picture of the Lee Abbey Youth Camp!

A disaster like this always causes people to question how a loving God can possibly allow such a horrific thing to happen. Why should some die and others be spared? It is one of the eternal mysteries to which the Christian can produce no simple solution. For Lee Abbey, the event was a very humbling reminder of the Lord's protection when faced by potential catastrophe.

Twice, the estate has been threatened by fire. It was the first day of the Easter Houseparty in 1956 when a fire began in the Valley of Rocks and advanced rapidly towards the estate. Fire brigades from miles around were called in to battle against the great walls of flame. As on all occasions of crisis, Leslie Sutton gathered together a group of people to pray that the fire might in no way harm the estate.

Only a few weeks previously the junior Chaplain, Ken

Pillar, had been married to Margaret. Top Lodge, which
stands at the entrance of the estate, was their first home. As
the fire was advancing, the fire officer told them that they
would have to evacuate the house and so with a number of
the Community they began to move everything out, stack-
ing all their possessions along the side of the road. But even
as people were passing things out of the upstairs windows to
load them onto the trailer, down below Leslie was carrying
them back in again through the front door, announcing that
they must have faith! The time came when the Fire Officer
said that it would no longer be safe to go back into the
house; suddenly the wind changed direction and the flames
began to move away from Lee Abbey and up the hillside. It
was an incredible sight for there was a semi-circle of flames
around the south-east of the estate, but at no point did the
fire come on to Lee Abbey property.

   Similar scenes were witnessed three years later, although
this time it was the main house that was threatened. A
group of Community members were returning along the
cliff path from Lynton, after a long walk on Exmoor, when
they saw smoke and flames coming from the cliff side ahead
of them. Their immediate reaction was that it was Lee
Abbey itself which was on fire, and it appeared that no one
was aware of what was happening. Quickly the alarm was
raised, and it was discovered that a fire was already well out
of control along the cliff to the north of the house.

   Some young boys who had been fishing at Lee Stone had
started a fire to cook their fish, but had not completely
extinguished it. The summar of 1959 had been very dry,
and by September all the vegetation was parched. The
tremendous heat produced by the fire was causing an
up-draught that was in turn drawing the flames up the cliff
side. All the able-bodied men of the Community and
among the guests helped the firemen tackle a very difficult
situation. There was no way of getting water to the area and
the only method of containing the fire was by beating and
hacking away at the undergrowth in front of it.

The situation was becoming increasingly serious. When the fire reached the path at the top of the cliff it would then be in the woods. From there, once it got hold of the tops of the trees it would quickly spread to the main house. The house was evacuated and the firemen played their hoses onto the trees surrounding the north lawn and the roof of the house to try to prevent any sparks from taking hold.

Once again it was to be Leslie, the man of faith, who rallied everyone to prayer. All those who were not involved in the actual fire fighting were summoned to the north lawn. Leslie led them in prayer that God would change the direction of the wind and would protect the house from harm. They looked up to see that the sparks were blowing not towards the house, but out to sea. The next day the Chief Fire Inspector commented, 'I don't have any particular faith, but it was a miracle that saved your building.' The progress of the fire had been halted by an increase in the off-shore wind, just as the flames had reached the top of the cliff.

Although it was possible for the guests now to return to their beds, that was not to be the end of the danger. The cliffs were to smoulder for over a week, and a constant watch was kept by the men of the Community day and night, to put out any small fires that flared up. In the very dry conditions the fire smouldered deep in the undergrowth, and quite unexpectedly a gorse bush would flare up. It was not until the rain came that they could be certain that there was no danger of another outbreak.

Thus Lee Abbey was spared from fire on two occasions. There is nothing remarkable about variations in the strength and direction of the wind, which changes all the time; but on both occasions the merciful alteration came at a critical moment, and when people were praying.

Not long after the Lynmouth flood disaster, there was another incident that clearly demonstrated God's protecting hand on Lee Abbey.

From the beginning there had been problems with the

roof of the octagonal lounge. Every time it rained, a whole collection of buckets would be needed to catch the drips. Something had to be done to rectify this situation. It was decided that the lounge should be re-roofed – the pitch of the roof should be increased, the lead taken off and replaced with felting. This involved removing the boarding, which revealed the main skeleton structure of roof timbers.

One Saturday morning while this work was in progress, Geoffrey and Dora were preparing to go to a meeting in Lynton in connection with the flood disaster. They had just got into the car when Geoffrey felt a strange compulsion that for some reason he must go and look at the work being done on the roof. So, dressed as he was, he ran upstairs, climbed out through the window that led on to the roof and saw that the workmen were in the process of replacing the boarding. As he looked more closely he saw that the roof was constructed out of two massive beams that spanned the entire room, and on which all the other timbers rested. In horror he noticed that in one place, one of these beams had rotted virtually the whole way through and was in danger of collapsing at any time. Already late for his meeting and with Dora waiting in the car, Geoffrey could not stay any longer so he gave hasty instructions to the workmen that they must find the foreman and do no more work at all on the roof until he returned.

With the meeting over, Geoffrey immediately went back up on to the roof to see what should be done. However, his instructions had been ignored and the boarding replaced. This time he took care that repairs were effected, the boarding removed again and the rotten beam made safe.

Of the 'Three Musketeers' Geoffrey was probably the one least accustomed to acting on impulse, yet if he had not obeyed his inner prompting to inspect the roof, Lee Abbey might well have been the scene of a most terrible tragedy, had the roof collapsed on a room filled with people.

The official opening, June, 1946

Pictured from left to right: Roger de Pemberton,
Cuthbert Bardsley, The Archdeacon of Barnstaple, The
Bishop of Exeter, The Vicar of Lynton, Leslie Sutton,
Jack Winslow, 'Tommy' Thompson

The North View of the house before 1967

The Chapel – c. 1955

Three Musketeers – Jack Winslow, Geoffrey Rogers, Leslie Sutton

Princess Wilhelmina plants a tree in the front of the house

'Pop' Hughes

The main house, 1981

The Octagonal Lounge, 1955

*The Lee Abbey International Students Club*

The Chapel

Edinburgh House

The Earl of March opens the Club

*The 21st Anniversary in the Royal Albert Hall*

Pictured from left to right: Cliff Richard; Donald Coggan, Archbishop of York; Cuthbert Bardsley, Bishop of Coventry; Ken Pillar

'Chapter 1975 – in the centre, Pam and Geoffrey Paul and Madelaine

The Youth Camp, 1978

The Lee Abbey Council, January, 1979

Community Folk Dancing in the
Back Yard.  In circle:
John and Gay Perry

An Outreach Team at the Devon
Show

# 10

# Community and Church

From the beginning it was realised that Lee Abbey should have a very special ministry to clergy. *Towards the Conversion of England* had pin-pointed the need for the English clergy, traditionally seen as pastors, to be trained for evangelism, and other concerns were also noted. It was a time when many were still on such pitifully small incomes that families who desperately needed a holiday from their parishes could never afford to take one. Then there were clergy who, having been in a post for a number of years, had become overtired, disheartened at the apparent lack of success and had lost much of their spiritual vision. As if this were not enough there were depressing trends in the Church; dwindling congregations, lack of manpower necessitating the amalgamation of parishes, and the general questioning of the role of the parish priest which had hitherto been unchallenged.

Within the first eight years it was estimated that over 1,000 clergy had stayed at Lee Abbey. They came for varied reasons. From the beginning there were those who were eager to be involved with Lee Abbey and its work. The Community were greatly encouraged when in the first winter of 1946–7 the Bishop of Truro arranged for a small group of his clergy to visit Lee Abbey to study evangelism with a member of his staff and the Community. As news of Lee Abbey began to spread, a number of clergy came out of sheer curiosity to see for themselves what was actually going on. Others came for no other reason than that it was a cheap, or at times, free holiday.

As finance was so often a crippling problem for clergy families, the Team decided that it would be right to invite, free of charge, a number of clergy with their wives to a clergy recess in the week following the Easter Houseparty – a good time for parochial clergy to take a break. This was once again a venture of faith, for the Community still needed as much money as possible to help clear the debts. Yet during the week itself a Friend who knew nothing of what was happening wrote saying that she felt guided to send a gift to Lee Abbey and enclosed a cheque for £200, sufficient to cover the whole cost of the week. Similar provision was to be made the following year. These clergy recesses became an annual event, and it was later necessary to run two successive weeks to cope with the demand.

These were by no means easy times. Some of the clergy were far from sympathetic with what they found at Lee Abbey. Many were confronted with the enigma of churchmanship. Jack Winslow's presence made the place acceptable to the Anglo-Catholics and Geoffrey Roger's to the evangelicals – but together? From normal parochial life, where the party lines were generally much more clearly drawn, it was hard to come to terms with what was found at Lee Abbey.

The visit of one clergyman was to be remembered by the Community for many years. On returning home after a clergy recess he telephoned the Community to tell them that he had been greeted by his daughter with 'Mummy, Daddy's come home with a new face!' A little girl's exclamation was able to explain what God had been doing far more clearly than any sermon. Her father, Arthur, was a curate in Ilfracombe. An invitation to a recess had been sent to his vicar. He, being rather suspicious of Lee Abbey, had deputed his curate to go in his place. Arthur was a firm Anglo-Catholic with a deep suspicion of other traditions.

The opening session had already begun as he arrived at Lee Abbey and his worst fears were soon confirmed: as he sat at the back of the octagonal lounge his face betrayed the fact that he was far from happy. Yet as the week progressed, he found that his suspicions were allayed by the atmosphere of warm fellowship. The party differences that had once been so prominent in his thinking became minor considerations in the light of the new relationship with God that he was experiencing. He returned home a changed man and it was to influence the whole of his ministry. The vicar was very impressed by all that he heard and as well as getting Arthur to write up the story in the parish magazine, he went to Lee Abbey himself when an invitation came the following year. Now instead of keeping a distance from the other clergy in the town, Arthur approached the local evangelical church to ask if he might share with them in the evangelistic services which were held on the sea front in the summer months.

With such a diverse group of clergy it might have been assumed that speakers would have to be careful in what they said. Yet there was no soft pedalling; what mattered was commitment to Christ. The continual stress was on the need for the Church to present a strong evangelistic message and to preach the necessity for personal conversion. It was inevitable that such an approach would receive a mixed reception, not only because of its theology, but because the clergy were challenged to consider their own commitment to Christ. One couple made their feelings very apparent by refusing to come into epilogues. As everybody settled down in the octagonal lounge, they would sit and read their newspapers in the small lounge. For three successive years they came to the recess without attending any talks, but gradually something was stirring within them. One night they propped the door open, and sat in the corridor just outside, surreptitiously listening to all that was being said. At the end of their third visit, as the couple were driving off, the wife suddenly wound down the car window and handed a note to Geoffrey, who was saying farewell to the guests. Quickly she wound the window up again and they drove away. The note read, 'I want to let you know that last night I gave my life to Christ. I went down onto the beach at Wringcliff bay and baptised myself in the stream that runs over the sand.'

It was to be the beginning of a whole new ministry for both of them.

Clergy, whose work calls them to offer help to others, are often the most reluctant to accept help for themselves. This has meant that some of the most outstanding clergy weeks have also, at times, been the most difficult. On several visits as guest speaker Agnes Sanford introduced the subject of the healing of memories. A few years later Frank Lake, with the subject of clinical theology, was helping clergy to understand themselves as a way of enriching their counselling ministries; for many this was a painful exercise.

Equally controversial, though in a different way, was the decision to invite Methodist ministers to join with the Anglicans for a joint recess in the autumn of 1965. The Anglican–Methodist unity commission had just been set up. There was great disappointment and frustration when the Bishop of Exeter stated that he would not give permission for the Methodist ministers to join in Holy Communion at the conference. Lee Abbey's practice of admitting non-Anglicans at Holy Communion had always been regarded with considerable suspicion in the Diocese. It seemed that the only answer to this problem would be to have no Communion services during the week, but merely an *agape* meal at the end. This was most unsatisfactory, for it caused Lee Abbey to emphasise the very disunity that it was seeking to heal. However, the Bishop subsequently rescinded his ruling, and granted permission for members of other Churches to join in Holy Communion at Lee Abbey whenever a conference was specifically aimed towards reunion. The numbers at that particular recess were disappointingly small, but it was an important breakthrough for the Diocese of Exeter. It seems extraordinary on reflection to note that it was not until 1968 that Methodist clergy were regularly invited to join in clergy recesses, and it was another three years before clergy of other denominations were finally included!

However, by this time the recesses had become only a shadow of their former selves. With the rise of a whole variety of conferences for clergy, an invitation to stay at Lee Abbey was no longer a great attraction. Only one recess was held each year, and even this was often difficult to fill. Popular speakers would draw larger numbers, but the Community had to realise that the needs of the clergy had changed: Lee Abbey's ministry to them had to change accordingly.

Now a steady stream of clergy continue to come to Lee Abbey, to houseparties, conferences and weekend breaks. The most pressing need of many clergy is for a holiday with their families, and special rates are offered to help make this possible. Others are seeking a time for spiritual reflection, which is less structured than a traditional retreat. Conferences are designed to enable clergy and laity to look together at issues of current concern.

Many ministers first visit Lee Abbey when they are still training at theological colleges. Since 1950 the Ordinands Conference, normally held in the first week of January, has been an annual event. It is a unique conference in that all the Anglican theological colleges are invited to send representatives, and in the last few years this has been extended to include the Free Church colleges and women candidates. The Community saw this ministry to ordinands as being at the very centre of the vision of Lee Abbey, and great care was taken to issue invitations and make the conference known. When an additional Chaplain was appointed in 1953 one of his tasks was to visit all the theological colleges to speak about the work of Lee Abbey. The result was that with very few exceptions, and often only because of a clash of dates with the beginning of the term, all the theological colleges were sending representatives. As with the clergy recesses, the conferences were often far from easy. Many ordinands came with deep suspicions of other traditions, which were not lightly shed. It seemed as if some were there because they had been sent, rather than by their own choice, and at one time it was considered unwise to indicate a person's college on his name badge! Yet this meeting together was invaluable. For some ordinands it was the first time that they had met and talked with someone from another tradition, and many came to appreciate others' insights. One practical repercussion was a request from the students to their college principals to begin an exchange scheme whereby several students would exchange colleges for a couple of weeks.

The mood of the Ordinands Conference has altered over the years. With just as many colleges represented, there is now no hint of the previous suspicions. One reason is perhaps that the average man accepted for training is older, so the majority are mature married men with families, but it is also further evidence of what the Holy Spirit is doing, bringing new unity and understanding in the Church.

For a number of Community members a time spent at Lee Abbey has been a preparation for the ordained ministry. Some have joined the Community with that idea in mind, to find it either confirmed or not during their stay. Others have never remotely considered the possibility of ordination, only to discover that this was the way in which the Lord was calling them to serve Him.

One former member of the Community, who was later to be ordained, described his time at Lee Abbey thus, 'I was like a very battered ship coming into dry dock, being scraped down and refurbished with new engines and new oil and then being launched slowly.' David had first come to Lee Abbey on a student working party in 1954. Three years later, after going through a bad period of depression, he returned as a working guest. His month's stay did not produce the immediate change for which he had been longing and so the time was extended. It was only after six months as a working guest that he felt able to accept the suggestion that he might become a member of the Community. For the next two years he worked with Ursula on the farm looking after the poultry. Slowly the experience of living in the Community, knowing the love and the care of the Body of Christ surrounding him, together with wise counselling from Jack, Leslie and Phyllis and also prayer when hands were laid on him, were to bring David the healing that he was seeking. He was also to discover that the Lord was giving him a ministry of healing, but it was not until his last couple of months that the idea of ordination became a real possibility to him. After being accepted for training he left the Community to spend six months working in Coventry before going to theological college. He was to be the fourth man in succession of those responsible for the poultry at Lee Abbey who went on to be ordained!

A number of clergy have returned with groups from their parishes and this ministry has emerged as one of the significant parts of Lee Abbey's work. Often it is only when a group from a church go away together that they begin to relate to each other. Barriers come down as the church warden is discovered in his dressing-gown desperately trying to get a cup of tea from a vending machine at seven-thirty a.m., or a member of the youth club is faced by an elderly spinster in a dance in which neither is quite sure of the steps! However, it is not merely that Lee Abbey offers suitable accommodation where a group can stay; what is more important is that a group is able to witness the life of a Christian community. Small details of Lee Abbey's daily life can leave big impressions. The fact that the farmer, not the Chaplain, is giving the evening epilogue; the evident care and support from fellow Community members for the highly nervous girl giving her testimony; the natural unity of a Baptist and high Anglican as they lead a pre-breakfast Bible study. For many groups, observing the way that the Community works raises big questions about their own life together.

Worshipping with the Community may also be a new experience. The form of service, and even the music, may be familiar, (though a full room with good acoustics – the octagonal lounge was built as a music room – does aid singing) but the key to different experiences is not in externals, but in the commitment of the people.

In the mid-sixties there was an important change in the pattern of Sunday worship at Lee Abbey. Instead of encouraging the guests to go into Lynton to attend Matins at the Parish Church, it was decided to hold a family Communion service in the octagonal lounge. Using the newly published Series Two service of Holy Communion (and later Series Three and the Alternative Service Book) this weekly service has enabled many people to gain a new experience of what is meant by worshipping together. With the table in the centre of the room, a circular seating pattern means that people are facing their fellow worshippers, rather than staring at the back of their heads. They are not merely told that they are the Body of Christ, they are able to feel it.

In this way many parish groups are given a taste of what their worship might be and return to seek ways of implementing what they have experienced in their own churches. It is, of course, here that frustration can come. A group will return eager to share what they have learned, to be met as often as not with indifference or even hostility. An individual in this situation can have little influence, but a group is far from helpless. The story of four young families, living near one another on a new housing estate, who visited Lee Abbey as a group in the summer of 1957 illustrates this.

One of them had visited Lee Abbey the previous year, and as a result of his experience then he began to play a much greater part in the life of his parish church. He became secretary of the P.C.C. and initiated a church fellowship to meet for discussion after the evening service. He brought in a Lee Abbey Friend to speak at the first meeting, and after further meetings managed to persuade a group to go to a houseparty the following year.

There was no church building on their housing estate, although plans for one were being considered. The curate from the parish church was living on the estate and held a monthly Communion service in a nearby public hall. An attempt had been made to reach the young families in the area: after a special house-to-house invitation a monthly family service had been started, and transport was provided as an encouragement to attend. But it had been a big flop. The first service was unattractive and discouraged congregational participation; the atmosphere was 'cold and unwelcoming', there was little to attract a newcomer and as a consequence few people came to the further services. Returning from their holiday at Lee Abbey the group were eager to be involved and suggested a Bible study and prayer group for the area, which the curate perhaps might be willing to lead. Much to their surprise and disappointment he showed little enthusiasm for their suggestion.

They were not to be easily deterred. At Lee Abbey the great truth which they had discovered was the need to pray and believe. They had even discussed the question of what Christians can do in a situation where their own clergy appear to be the main obstacle to the free working of the Holy Spirit. The confident reply had been, 'Pray about them and they will either change or leave within six months.' At the time they had wondered whether this advice was seriously intended.

With the consent of the vicar a group did begin to meet for prayer and Bible study, and within four months the curate had left. The situation on the housing estate was now wide open to new possibilities. Members of the group took the lead in establishing a number of organisations: a boys' Bible class, a young wives' group and Sunday schools meeting in ordinary homes led by members of the praying group. However, the greatest need was for a new curate who could live on the estate and lead the work. Week by week they prayed but with no apparent answer. As their confidence began to sag a letter from Leslie Sutton brought new encouragement, 'The group must persist in faith – with one heart – receiving such a man from God – praying for the bishop.' They persisted in prayer and again the weeks went by. Eventually a man was found. He was about to be married and his present parish could not afford to retain his services as curate. He was very clearly the man of God's choice.

With his arrival regular services were held each Sunday in the public hall and received increasing support. The running was not altogether smooth, however, for there was bitter opposition to the new ministry from the local church committee. It was only through the curate's own personal courage and the prayerful support of the group that his enthusiasm for the work was unaffected.

In spite of many difficulties, the work continued to expand as people were converted and new Christians moved into the area. The prayer group became so large that it had to subdivide, and the congregation outgrew the hall which was eventually replaced by a permanent church building. A new fellowship had been established, because a small group had learned at Lee Abbey the power of believing prayer.

It is one thing to talk about faith in God among the glorious scenery in North Devon, and another to have to work it out in a typical industrial parish. If Lee Abbey is to be seen as having something to say about parish life, then it must be from first-hand experience. Responsibility for Exmoor village churches like Barbrook and Martinhoe and varying degrees of involvement in St. Mary's, Lynton, provide a very limited experience of normal parish problems. From the beginning it was realised that Lee Abbey's ministry was going to have to be a two-way process. In the second issue of the Lee Abbey newsletter in 1946 the

Chaplain, Tommy Thompson, described a visit that he and Leslie had made to different churches in the Midlands.

> I believe that this tour is a forerunner of many such excursions from Lee Abbey to help forward the work in local situations. The battle is fought in places where men live and work and have their being. Lee Abbey exists to serve the parishes. There must be a constant interplay between the two. It will be right for you to bring parties to Lee Abbey next year to the houseparties to be arranged for such groups. Equally, it will be right for us to visit you, bringing perhaps a small team from the Community to give your work a 'boost'.

It was an accurate prediction of the way in which Lee Abbey now works. Almost every year the winter programme has included a couple of teams from the Community going out all over England to share in parish missions. The form of the missions has changed with the general trend – away from the days of the nightly mission meeting in the parish hall with singing and a main speaker, towards a greater emphasis on informal home meetings, concluding with a final challenge service.

For Community members such visits always provide a great encouragement as they discover the Holy Spirit's resources for tasks thought impossible. Although missions in no way make the Community expert in parochial problems, they are a good reminder of the situations faced by many of the guests. The greatest value is in witnessing how Community life works out in a parish setting.

Every team is led by a Chaplain and includes several senior Community members, but the rest of the team is made up of young members of the Community for whom this is a totally new experience. Unlike other groups who normally undertake missions, from theological colleges, traditional communities or the Church Army, they have limited expertise. However, in many parishes it is this

evident weakness which makes the impact, for here are
ordinary Christians with whom it is easy to identify. During
a Lee Abbey mission the challenge is not only to the
uncommitted to accept the living Christ; it is also to the
committed as they are called to face what is really involved
in being part of the fellowship of the Holy Spirit. One vicar
from a parish near Southampton commented in a letter
after a celebration week,

> A number of people came to commit themselves to the
> Lord as a result of the week and we are seeing them in
> services and fellowships. That is cause for real thankful-
> ness and joy to us. But undoubtedly the main blessing
> has been in the church. Certainly the P.C.C. has a fresh
> enthusiasm and a vision of what we ought to be doing.
> Having seen the team with shy members in it, a vision of
> what we can do ourselves. It had to be seen to be
> believed. I think it is significant that the Lord used the
> togetherness of a very mixed team as much as He used
> the individual conversations.

# 11

## Further Afield

Is Lee Abbey a place in North Devon, a community of people, or a movement within the Church?

This question has been debated many times and it was in the background of much of the discussion in the Lee Abbey Council during the fifties. The issue was whether God was calling the Council to establish centres in other parts of the country to extend the work of the original vision.

Once the work in Devon had become securely established the Council no longer had to spend all their time on the administrative details, which had been essential in the early years. So while continuing to keep a close watch on all that was happening they were able to explore other possibilities. Some members of the Council were anxious that Lee Abbey should proliferate – a house near Lynton was only one of many centres that they might possibly establish.

Two ideas were debated at the annual Council Conference in January 1953. They were the establishment of a training centre, and 'a London house'. Although particular weeks had been set aside for training, this aspect of Lee Abbey's original vision, as a centre for lay training, had never been fulfilled. Before the construction of the motorway system Lee Abbey was too remote for people to be able to reach for a weekend. The only specific training courses were two weekends organised each winter by the Community at Rosehill, near Reading, to provide follow-up teaching in the Christian life for those who had been to summer houseparties. Later these were extended to Swan-

wick and High Leigh, but what was really needed was a
centre, somewhat smaller than Lee Abbey and easily ac-
cessible from London, which could be used to run training
courses both at weekends and mid-week.

The majority of Lee Abbey guests came from the Home
Counties, and the other need that was continually being
voiced was for a Lee Abbey centre in London itself. Clearly
it would be supported. The monthly meetings held at
the Royal Empire Society in the winter months were
attracting up to five hundred people to listen to challenging
messages from speakers like Cuthbert Bardsley and Wallace Bird. If there were a permanent centre, it could
become a rallying point for Lee Abbey Friends, a place for
planning and prayer, and a base for training. The idea was
very attractive. It was also a real possibility, as two properties, which appeared to be most suitable for these purposes, had been offered to the Council.

After investigations neither property proved to be right.
The Council continued to explore the idea of setting up a
training centre and over the next few years a number of
enquiries were made and several places visited, yet none
was suitable. The idea of establishing a London centre
raised a fundamental issue. It would meet a real need, but it
could also prove counter-productive to Lee Abbey's aims.
The challenge to guests at houseparties was that they
should return home and become committed to the life of
their local church. There was a danger that a permanent
London centre could become a substitute for those dis-
satisfied with their own church. A highly suitable property
which had been offered was a flat in a London vicarage, but
on reflection it was considered most undesirable that any
one church should become identified as a 'Lee Abbey'
church, and so become a 'Mecca' for Lee Abbey Friends in
the London area. Ten years later a London centre was to be
opened, but it was to be very different from anything
envisaged at this time.

There were also plenty of people who were eager to see

the establishment of other places doing similar work to that of Lee Abbey in Devon, running holiday houseparties. A number of the Council, including Geoffrey, were very cautious of this idea. Although it was clear that God was richly blessing the work in Devon, there was no guarantee that a similar venture in another part of the country would be successful. It was a complex series of factors that God had brought together; there were the Community, the leadership, and the beauty of the setting, and none of this could be duplicated automatically in another place.

The strongest move for another Lee Abbey came from the North of England. As early as June 1948 Jack had written in the newsletter that 'I have always thought that some place similar to Lee Abbey must in due course be established somewhere in the North, to meet the needs of those who can hardly be expected to come all the way to Devon from there.' The Council did not then feel it right to take any active steps to investigate this possibility. In 1957, a group of Lee Abbey Friends from the North of England took the initiative to circulate some 700 Friends in that area asking for their response to the possibility of 'founding in the North an instrument for the revival of the Church, perhaps a Community of the same general character as Lee Abbey.'

From the strength of the replies they decided actively to pursue this idea. Already a possible property had been discovered: another Lee Abbey Friend, Bernard Jacob, was taking part in a mission at Skipton. Talking to his hosts about Lee Abbey and his longing to see such a place in the North of England, his attention was drawn to a nearby property that was being advertised for sale, Scargill House, situated near the village of Kettlewell in Wharfedale.

The initial reaction of the Council was not favourable to the proposal. The Team at Lee Abbey did not feel it was worth the journey to visit the house; it was too small to be economic, and was situated in the wrong place. They were to change their minds when they saw the beautiful location for themselves.

Events moved much more swiftly than the Council had envisaged, and in November an agreement was signed at Middleton Rectory in Manchester by a small group, chaired by Donald Coggan, Bishop of Bradford, to purchase Scargill House. As in the purchase of Lee Abbey it was a great act of faith; the group had committed themselves to raising £20,000 in gifts or loans within two months.

With the decision taken, the Lee Abbey Council were anxious to support the venture in every way possible though realising that they were not to be responsible for the work, as they had initially assumed. A letter was sent out to interested people including all the Lee Abbey Friends with news of the new scheme and explaining the financial needs. It received a remarkable response. Within the two months over £42,000 had been offered as gifts or as loans; a sufficient sum both for the purchase of the property and to enlarge and equip the house.

Although Scargill has always been totally independent of Lee Abbey, the close spiritual affinity that exists between the two Communities was demonstrated at the official Dedication on June 27th 1959, which was conducted by Cuthbert Bardsley, Bishop of Coventry and chairman of the Lee Abbey Council. A visitor to Scargill, having stayed at Lee Abbey, may soon observe that the pattern of life and ministry adopted by the Scargill Community reflects a number of features pioneered at Lee Abbey, but there are also a number of notable differences. For example the idea of the Team or Chapter, which has always been considered to be the heart of Lee Abbey's administration, has never been adopted at Scargill. Also, being situated close to the heart of industrial England, near Leeds and Bradford, Scargill has been able to establish from the beginning a special ministry to industrial and secular groups.

When Scargill was opened, Lee Abbey had been established for fourteen years and was clearly enjoying considerable success. Guests were flocking to houseparties so that many applicants had to be disappointed; the work was now based on a sound financial footing. Money was not plentiful, but neither was it a problem; the policy was to keep the fees as low as possible while still covering running expenses. Behind the work was the concerned backing of a large company of Friends.

The atmosphere within the Church of England had also greatly changed. The fifties had been a time of encouragement, highlighted by the visits of Billy Graham. His methods were inevitably controversial, yet he managed to reach the general public of the country with the Gospel, in a way that no Church or other individual had managed to do for many years. The great crusades at Harringay in London made a profound impact on the Church. Some people wished to dismiss the crusades as being based purely on emotionalism, but time proved otherwise. The crusades engendered a new sense of urgency and enthusiasm in many clergy and lay people for evangelism. Many regular church attenders found themselves 'converted' and now living as evangelical Christians in non-evangelical and often anti-evangelical churches. For the Church of England the lasting impact of the crusades was the number of men who, tracing the beginning of their spiritual life to the crusades, later offered themselves for ordination. Many people whose lives had been touched at the crusades visited Lee Abbey to find teaching and encouragement. No longer could the Community feel alone in the work of seeking to promote evangelism within the Church of England.

This renewed concern for evangelism meant that Lee Abbey was becoming far more acceptable within the establishment of the Church, compared with the times when it was either unknown or aroused considerable suspicion. No less than five members of the Council were bishops. At the annual thanksgiving service in 1960, Geoffrey Fisher, Archbishop of Canterbury, was present. The words that he spoke in St. Paul's Cathedral before he gave the blessing, demonstrated to the Community and to the Church Lee Abbey's acceptance within the establishment.

'I have for long included Lee Abbey among the works of the Church for which I praise God; and I have praised Him with increasing certainty and happiness as time has gone on. Today I have seen something of your spirit and of your fellowship. I have received from you new refreshment and encouragement in the service of the Lord, from your numbers here gathered, from your voices raised in prayer and praise. I praise the Lord with you, have magnified His name together with you. I shall be able now with even greater sincerity and confidence to thank God for you, your witness and your work.'

Here was the evidence that God had honoured the faith of the founders, as Lee Abbey enjoyed spiritual and material success. But it was a situation that was fraught with danger. Lee Abbey was born as a venture of faith, but now there was no longer the need for the daring faith which had to depend on God alone for material and spiritual needs. The pioneering days were over and there was a temptation to see the task as maintaining a proven system and style ministry. Leslie, in particular, sensed the danger of complacency. In his message to the Friends at the start of the new decade he wrote, 'Though we humbly thank God for all His blessings since 1945, we are terribly aware that we, the Lee Abbey Friends, need a new vision and an anointing of the fire of God's love if ever we are to meet in any degree the challenge of the world's desperate need in 1960.'

During the sixties Lee Abbey was to face the turmoil and upheaval that confronted the whole Church, but other changes would also occur within the Community itself. In 1960 the ministry of the Three Musketeers, who had been at the heart of Lee Abbey for the last ten years, was drawing to a close.

In 1958 Leslie had suffered a severe coronary thrombosis, and had been in Barnstaple Hospital for three months. Although he made a good recovery it was clear to both him and Phyllis that their time on the Community was limited and that they should be seeking a less demanding ministry. Jack was seventy-eight, and although still very active, thinking nothing of leading a 23-mile Doone Valley walk, would clearly not be able to continue much longer.

Over the years the chaplaincy team had been built up, so that it was now customary to have two younger ordained men on the Community in addition to Jack. This team was further supplemented by the arrival of Kristeen MacNair. She had served with the China Inland Mission and had recently completed her training for parish work. She was the first woman Chaplain.

Later that same year, 1960, Leslie and Phyllis were offered a flat in Farnborough and retired from Lee Abbey to continue an active ministry together, especially among Lee Abbey Friends, until Leslie's death in 1968. They were succeeded by Gordon and Sheila Mayo and their family, who had just returned to England after spending ten years working with the Christian Council in Kenya. These replacements among the Team and other senior Community members inevitably brought change; new people were able to look at Lee Abbey through different eyes and spark off new ideas.

As a direct result there was considerable debate about the nature and the purpose of the Community. Until 1960 the position had never been questioned. Lee Abbey had been founded as a centre for lay training and evangelism; the purpose of the Community was to serve the guests – without the guests, the Community had no significance.

Now several people, like Kristeen and Gordon and Sheila, felt that the Community should be seen as having significance in itself. After different experiences of community life overseas they were attracted to Lee Abbey partly by the exciting possibilities of further exploring the Christian life in a community. They believed that Lee Abbey, in addition to its ministry to guests, was an important experiment by God, which had much to teach the whole Church.

This subject was discussed at length both in the Team and in Community meetings. There was a tendency to reduce the debate to a straight choice between two contrasting positions. Was Lee Abbey a 'guest house' staffed by resident members, living as a community, or a Christian community which opened its doors to share its life and home with other people? This over-simplification seemed to sum up the difference between the first and second generation at Lee Abbey. Geoffrey, as one of the founders, was anxious that the place should not become introspective, preoccupied with itself, and so lose its cutting edge as an agent of mission. For others the mission of Lee Abbey consisted not merely in what it said or did, but in what it was, and there was a danger of being so preoccupied with activity centred around the guests, that the life of the Community suffered.

It was a debate that produced no clear-cut solution; rather it highlighted a healthy tension, with which the Community continues to live. The problem is not unique to Lee Abbey but has to be faced by any community that is essentially 'task orientated' and indeed by any local church congregation. Has God placed us in a certain situation 'to be' or 'to do'? A balanced Christian life will have to hold these two together.

# 12

# The Chapter of Friends

Jack had been reading the recently published *Life of St. Francis* by Elizabeth Goudge. At the weekly Team meeting, he shared with the senior members of the Community something that had caught his imagination. This was the description of the 'Chapter of Mats' held at Assisi in 1219.

Frances had preached on a minstrel's chant;

> Great things we have promised,
> But greater are promised to us.
> What we have promised let us fulfill,
> To what we are promised let us look forward.
> A brief delight and punishment forever;
> A little suffering and glory infinite.

Jack saw the obvious implications that this had for Lee Abbey, and he proposed that there should be a 'Chapter of Friends', a calling together of the Lee Abbey Friends, just like the early Franciscans, to wait upon God and seek His will for the future.

Both the Team at Lee Abbey and the Council welcomed Jack's proposal and detailed plans were laid for the Chapter to be held at Lee Abbey from September 9th to 16th, 1961. Gordon Mayo was responsible for the vast administration involved. The plan was to bring together some five hundred Friends, most of whom would have to be accommodated in guest houses and hotels in and around Lynton. Jack stated that the purpose of the week was to renew the spiritual life of the whole company of Friends, lifting it to a higher level and also to see if God was challenging them to new action.

May we not hope that, just as the Chapter of Mats led the Franciscans to new and more daring adventures for Christ, so at our Chapter of Friends God may call us to some new enterprise, some further outreach, which will counter any temptation to rest upon our oars, and enable us to be of wider service to God, to the work of his Kingdom?

In preparation for the Chapter, Friends were asked to write in with ideas of how they believed God might be leading Lee Abbey and the Friends.

There was a ready response. Friends were involved in a wide variety of Christian and secular service, and here was the opportunity to relate that to Lee Abbey. Subjects ranging from vivisection to lay training were covered in the many background papers for the Chapter. A number of common themes emerged. There was the desire to find an expression of deeper commitment to Christ. Could Lee Abbey establish a 'third Order'? What about lay training? Lee Abbey was a centre for evangelism and lay training, but many felt the lay training aspect was hardly touched upon. This was one of the desperate needs of the Church. Could a programme of lay training conferences be organised throughout the year, perhaps at a number of local centres? Could Lee Abbey have a team to go into parishes, perhaps with caravans, to conduct training weekends? Perhaps clergy who had come to the annual recesses could be trained also to conduct such weekends. Could a residential centre be established to concentrate on this training?

There was a definite proposal that Lee Abbey should establish a residential youth centre, to train young people for leadership and evangelism. Max Warren, the General Secretary of C.M.S., who had recently returned from a world tour, wrote to encourage Lee Abbey to consider seriously the need in Australia for a centre which would be a focus for spiritual renewal. He also suggested the need for something like Lee Abbey in Nigeria, where the Church needed a greater awareness of evangelism.

From this mass of preparatory documents, two papers had a profound effect upon the Chapter. One of them was from Mrs Louise Locke.

Louise had first come to Lee Abbey as a guest in 1949, when she was going through a very bleak time. She was suffering from bad health, her marriage was going wrong, and she had just moved into a house with ten rooms that was far too big for her. She had not been near a church for ages and did not care about religion at all. After a long talk with a member of the houseparty, she found herself standing up on the final evening to share with the other guests how she felt that 'a great load had gone from her shoulders'.

The following year she returned with her children, and although she felt much happier, her health was still very poor. It was suggested that she might receive prayer with the laying on of hands; subsequently her health improved greatly.

She still had the problem of her over-large house. She had advertised for lodgers with no response until she received an unexpected telephone call. She described it thus:

It was from Miss Hilda Porter, from the Methodist International House, asking me if I would take coloured students, as she said someone who wished to remain anonymous had told her that I not only wanted boarders, but that I would be the right person to look after these students. I said 'no' at first as I said I had never spoken to a coloured person and I was still afraid of people, but Miss Porter persuaded me to take my first girl. This was Pushpa, a very young Indian girl from Singapore who wanted to study Law. She was very charming. Pushpa said to me one day, 'I shall be twenty-one next week,' so I said that we had better have a tea party, and she said that she had no friends but in the end asked if she could ask a lonely Nigerian student to tea – I said yes. He was Igwe from Eastern Region. While he was with us he said it was nice to be inside a home so I told him he could come again, and suggested that he came any Saturday for tea and bring a friend over. One Saturday I came home with the children from shopping and found seven Nigerians on the doorstep. I took them all in and gave them some tea and decided there and then to have tea parties on Sundays.

Thus began Louise's ministry to overseas students. It was not long before three bedrooms at her home in Tooting were constantly available as accommodation for students, and she would try to find accommodation for others through the local papers and the churches. She began monthly coffee evenings in her home which soon outgrew the house and had to be moved to a nearby hall. A newspaper reporter, fascinated by Louise's work, noted the carefully written notice on a bookcase in her sitting room: 'Unless everybody present understands your language – it's only common politeness to speak English!' She worked hard to bring the needs of overseas students to the attention of the churches of all denominations, and formed 'The Balham and Tooting International Circle'. The British Council heard about her and she began to work with them in local accommodation campaigns, and in sending out letters of welcome to some 1,000 overseas students each year. In response she received many requests for help and advice and sought to link up the students with churches. She writes of this time: 'My work went on and on, and miracle after miracle happened – the main one being that Our Lord took over and gave me (a) education, (b) courage and the power of speech, (c) money when it was short and (d) the love of human beings.' She had tried to attract other Lee Abbey Friends to her work, often through the newsletter. Friends were encouraged to invite students to their homes and she also arranged for a number of students to come down and stay at Lee Abbey. Her close contacts with the Methodists and Roman Catholics meant that Louise greatly admired much that they were doing for students through their hostels, and she longed to see her own Church of England showing a similar practical concern. So it was that when she received the request for ideas in preparation for the Chapter of Friends, Louise prepared a paper setting out a scheme for a Lee Abbey Hostel in London for overseas students, which could also serve as a meeting place for Lee Abbey Friends.

Louise was not alone in her concern for overseas students. Another paper submitted to the Chapter on this subject came from Lt. Col. George Grimshaw, a former missionary who was working in the Overseas Visitors Department of C.M.S. In many ways his proposal was more ambitious than Louise's. He outlined his vision of a Christian Institute founded on an evangelical foundation with a residential nucleus of students and Community. There were over 25,000 overseas students living in London, and although many bodies were seeking to help them he was very conscious that there was not as yet any centre providing club facilities; it could organise seminars for groups of Christians; provide a Christian setting for meeting political and commercial leaders from overseas and introducing them to their Christian opposite numbers in this country; and provide a Christian 'intelligence centre' for some of the many uncoordinated and often unknown Christian cells of activity. From his experience with C.M.S. George was very clear that the work must be undergirded by a resident Community of Christians working and praying together.

With a real sense of expectation over five hundred of the Lee Abbey Friends finally assembled in a large marquee erected on the north lawn for the Chapter, with its title 'Task for Tomorrow'. The tone for the whole week was set by Jack as he preached at the opening service in the packed

Church of St. Mary's, Lynton, reiterating the words of Francis, 'What He has promised, let us fulfill – and to what we are promised, let us look forward.' Each day began with a Bible-reading by Wallace Bird on 'The Kingdom of the Spirit', then sessions and discussion groups looked at the changing situations facing the nation and the Church. Each evening 'Meeting Point' provided a forum for everybody to listen to many of the ideas that had been expressed in the preparatory papers being expounded.

Throughout the week the weather was generally very pleasant, but the wind blew as strongly as it can on the North Devon coast in the autumn. Indeed at times it looked as if it might lift the marquee off the ground. There were many Friends who were not slow to interpret this wind as a powerful sign from God of what He was wishing to do, not merely for Lee Abbey and the Friends, but for His whole Church.

As a result of the week a whole new area opened up for the mission of God through Lee Abbey. Few people can have gone away from the Chapter without the call to deeper commitment to Christ, His Church and the local community still ringing in their ears. Reports later evidenced this being worked out in practice. And at Lee Abbey itself, the Team and the Council were left with a list of seven recommendations requiring discussion and action.

The next meeting of the Council began the enormous task of deciding how to implement these suggestions, but most of them were to founder and come to nothing. There was the proposal for a residential youth centre which had been so strongly canvassed before the Chapter but which never got off the ground for lack of available leadership. Detailed plans were laid in conjunction with 'Christian Team Work' to establish a Friends Liaison office in London, but this too never worked out. Geoffrey did visit Nigeria in September 1963 to explore the possibility of establishing a sister house, but it was very clear that this would not be right.

One recommendation, however, that both the Team and the Council felt compelled by God to pursue, was that involving overseas students. So a fact-finding committee, including Louise Locke and George Grimshaw and chaired by Gordon Mayo, was set up to look at the possibilities.

In close co-operation with Christian Team Work, the next year was spent in assessing the whole situation concerning overseas students resident in London, and the possible options open to Lee Abbey. There was plenty to encourage them. In 1961 the Government had announced that they were willing to make up to three million pounds available to voluntary bodies for capital expenditure on projects concerned with Commonwealth young people. Quite clearly the funds would be provided if a project was undertaken. This money was made available through OSWEP (Overseas Students Welfare Extension Programme) and was administered by the British Council. The grant was interest-free, did not need to be repaid, and would be written off over a period of twenty-five years. In addition, the London County Council was also willing to offer mortgages for such projects at a fixed rate of interest, though this of course did have to be repaid. How different from the founding of Lee Abbey in Devon in 1945!

The committee also had the task of bringing together the two visions that had been outlined by George Grimshaw and Louise Locke at the Chapter. Two plans of action emerged. Firstly, Friends should be encouraged to establish hostels in their local area, on similar lines to Louise's work in Balham. These hostels would be their own responsibility, financially and administratively, and not Lee Abbey's. Secondly, Lee Abbey should go ahead and establish a much larger hostel near the centre of London, run by a Community, which would offer facilities as an International Centre.

So in 1963 the hunt was on to find suitable premises before starting the complicated legal procedures necessary to obtain available grants. The committee, now chaired by

Prebendary Denis Wakeling, were on the look-out for either a suitable site on which they could build a hostel, or existing property which they could adapt to their needs. One site in Wallace Bird's parish in Kennington seemed to be a real possibility, and a redundant church in Battersea was examined but both came to nothing.

Then one day in the autumn two letters arrived at Lee Abbey. One was from a Friend who knew all about the hostel project. He had been walking through Courtfield Gardens, off the Earls Court Road in Kensington, and had seen 'For Sale' boards outside several adjacent hotels. The other letter, also from a Lee Abbey Friend, drew attention to the same hotels which were being advertised in the Daily Telegraph. When it was discovered that the vicar of St. Jude's, Courtfield Gardens, was a Lee Abbey Friend, and Madeleine remembered that her uncle and aunt used to worship there, it was clear that this was a possibility to be pursued.

George Grimshaw was contacted and went to view the property. There were three separate hotels, Courtfield, Melbourne and Edinburgh, imposing Victorian buildings with white stucco fronts. They were within a short walking distance of each other and had been run as one establishment by the Overseas Visitors Club, an organisation providing accommodation mainly for white South Africans and Australians staying in London. As South Africa left the Commonwealth, so the club had gone out of business. The hotels were to be sold fully equipped down to the last detail, with the furnishings in Edinburgh virtually unused. The three properties were to be sold separately; they were almost ideal for what Lee Abbey had in mind.

As the day for the auction came, a vigil of prayer was arranged by the Community in the chapel. Frequent telephone calls were made between London and Devon as the day proceeded. The first hotel to be auctioned, Edinburgh, was purchased. The next call brought shattering news – Melbourne had been lost. It had gone above the agreed limit. Without the three together the project would not work, and so Lee Abbey's agent did not bid for Courtfield. It was withdrawn, as it did not reach its reserve. At the last moment, when all the indications had been positive, had God suddenly said 'no' to the project?

Within twenty-four hours this mood of disappointment had been turned to real rejoicing. Negotiations had taken place between the different agents involved and the purchaser of Melbourne was willing to let Lee Abbey have the property for the price he had paid; then Courtfield was obtained as well.

The next couple of months were to be ones of frantic activity. Lee Abbey had the property, which needed far less adaptation than anyone had imagined. So the work of accommodating students could begin almost as soon as the legal formalities had been completed. It had always been part of the project that Gordon Mayo was the obvious person to be the first Warden of the Lee Abbey International Students Club, as it was to be called. The same Chapter meeting also agreed that three of the department leaders (Lily Dear, the Secretary, Mary Hope, the Head Cook, and Chris Mail, the House Leader) should go with Gordon and Sheila to form the nucleus of the London Community. The loss of so many key senior people at one time was to create a big gap in the Community in Devon but once again these were pioneering days.

Because the legal work had still to be completed, it was as caretaker rather than Warden that Gordon, with the other four, moved to London in January 1964. The property consisted of six houses, all of which were leasehold with six different original owners. The purchase was extremely complex and a lawyer's paradise! To begin with, the basement of Melbourne House became their headquarters as the London Community began the enormous task of cleaning and preparing the place for students. Much of the time had to be spent in cleaning Courtfield, which housed the main kitchen, as it had been used as the restaurant for the club. The scene must have been very reminiscent of the early days in Devon as the Community, together with a very enthusiastic band of local Lee Abbey Friends, set about attacking layers of accumulated grease and dirt – a task made the more difficult by the lack of any central heating or running hot water. A few days after they had arrived, George Grimshaw came to visit and brought some forsythia from his garden. 'If this doesn't come out into bloom here, we'll know it's too cold for you!' Much to some people's amazement, it did.

It was decided that the Community and students would live together in the three houses. The planned accommodation was for 180 students: 100 from Commonwealth countries, 30 from other countries, with the rest from Britain. The British Council were only too delighted to be able to direct recently arrived students to a new hostel.

The buildings had cost £236,000. The combined O.S.W.E.P. grant and the L.C.C. mortgage meant that only £6,000 had to be found by Lee Abbey itself. However, these grants were made on the security of the deeds of the Lee Abbey estate, and immediately an appeal was launched to the Lee Abbey Friends so that the deeds might be released as quickly as possible.

It would be hard to imagine two more contrasting places than Lynton and Earls Court, but both were now to be home for the two parts of the Lee Abbey Community. Here was to be the great test for the Community life that had evolved over the last nineteen years, as the London Community sought to express a corporate life in this urban multi-racial setting. It was not easy.

# 13

# Lee Abbey in London

We have over twenty nationalities now and the comments and reactions are very interesting. Our Yugoslavian doctor who has done a doctorate in languages (Persian included) but whose English is rather less than perfect told Pauline the other night that he admired her structure! He stands at the counter in the kitchen and says in a pathetic voice, 'How to be happy? You are happy. Why?' Margaret Njoke, our Kikuyu member, told him of Jesus which to him meant *nothing*. Jesus? Who is that? Meanwhile we try to live the sort of life which speaks louder than sermons. Our charming Muslim (one of the many) Yusufu Mohammed, from Northern Nigeria, asked to take his shoes off in the chapel and I think considered us as second-class religious because we only pray three times a day!

It was just over a month since Melbourne House had started to receive students and Sheila wrote, with real excitement, to the Community back in Devon.

They soon discovered that there was no shortage of students seeking accommodation. The temptation was to take too many before there were enough Community members to staff the place. As the Community grew in numbers so Courtfield came into use and finally Edinburgh, so that by the autumn the International Students Club had reached its full capacity of 180 students from 39 different

countries and six different religions, about two-thirds being
Christians.

The small Community of twenty-one members had much
to learn. For instruction in the actual mechanics of running
the place, a great deal of help was received from the
established overseas student hostels like William Temple
House and the Methodist International House. For their
Community life they adopted the same pattern of structure
and worship as in Devon, with probationary and full members, Community prayers each morning, Community intercessions and the weekly corporate Communion. In place of
red and green labels, which it was thought would be totally
out of place in a residential hostel, they had a distinctive
lapel badge. It was an ancient Egyptian symbol discovered
by Gordon and Sheila, a small anchor cross. As the main
dining room in Courtfield had many nautical trappings and
was called the Compass Room, it seemed a natural symbol
for the Community to adopt.

Part of one of John Donne's poems ('To Mr George
Herbert, with one of my seals, of the anchor and Christ')
emphasises the significance of the anchor cross:

> The Crosse (my seal at Baptism) spred below,
> Does, by that form, into an Anchor grow.
> Crosses grow Anchors; Bear, as thou shouldst do
> Thy Crosse, and that Crosse grows an Anchor too.
> But he that makes our Crosses Anchors thus,
> Is Christ, who there is crucified for us.

Although much of the basic structure of Community life
could be transferred to London, it soon became apparent
that their task was very different. The assumption had
always been that the London Community would relate to
the students in much the same way as the Devon Community did to the guests: this was not so. In Devon the house is
home for the Community; the guests come for their brief
stay and then leave. At the Club the students are the

residents, many staying up to three years, much longer than the majority of Community members. In Devon the relationship was that of hosts to guests; in London it was management to residents. It was essential that the students, who were not necessarily Christians, should be consulted and involved in the running of the Club.

The Community were not merely endeavouring to express the life of Lee Abbey in London; what was more important was for them to work out its mission. Initially there were those, including some Council members, who assumed that the London Club would be like Lynton with regular teaching sessions and evening 'evangelistic epilogues'. Unease had been expressed when it was learned that the British Council grant was dependent upon an undertaking that there would be no proselytising. Clarification revealed that this referred to compulsion for people to change their religion, which was not what Lee Abbey understood by evangelism! Through staying at the Club some students became Christians, testifying to their new-found faith through baptism and confirmation. This brought deep joy to the Community, but it was not the primary purpose of the Club. Evangelism was seen much more in terms of being a Christian presence, rather than simply making converts; leading the kind of life and saying the kind of things that allowed the Good News of Christ to become evident. The task of the Community in the Club was parallel to the task of the Church in the whole world, to live and witness in a society of many faiths and of none. After four years of ministry in London, Gordon used Jesus' picture of salt and light from the Sermon on the Mount to describe their mission. 'Salt, rather like yeast, is scattered into the environment it is meant to influence and gets thoroughly mixed up in it. Light, on the other hand, has to be positioned very carefully and obviously to be of any value. This dual role of the Christian has to be lived by the Community members under "glasshouse" conditions, for nothing that goes on misses the eyes of the students.'

The Community came to realise that God was calling them to witness in three major areas; their work, their life and worship, and their words. The first was in the provision of good-quality hostel accommodation. This was easier said than done. At the very first residents' meeting, the obvious forum for student complaints, Gordon was earnestly promising everyone that all the small repairs that needed doing would be attended to as quickly as possible, when a flood from a bathroom on the fourth floor began to pour down! Erratic plumbing and the antiquated central heating system caused a steady stream of complaints. A more serious problem was a major outbreak of dry rot in both Courtfield and Edinburgh, which not only disrupted life for everybody for months with the noise and upheaval of builders, but also placed a heavy financial burden on the Club, which had little surplus money. One consequence was that many normal repairs and renewals had to be postponed. When it had opened, with its maroon carpets and new furnishings, the Club offered some of the best-appointed student accommodation in London, but as the years went by it gradually became worn and shabby and was increasingly difficult to keep clean and attractive. It was not an easy environment for those who were being called to witness to Christ by the quality of their work.

It also proved a perplexing form of witness for the students. Many of them came from countries where it was impossible to conceive of the people in authority as also being the servants. It was hard to grasp that the people who ran and, as they assumed, owned the place, were also those who did the basic domestic work; cleaning lavatories, answering the telephone or cooking the meals. Here was one of the revolutionary features of the Christian faith – Jesus came to serve, not to be served.

The Community were not only providing a place to live, but also a home. Some students would come and stay at the Club for a few months after first arriving in Britain and then move on once they had found a flat or other accommodation. Others would stay for several years. For many it could be lonely and bewildering living in London, a society which had little time for students and especially for those from overseas who were often made to feel that they were parasites, living off another country. They needed a place where they could feel accepted, whatever their race or religion, where they would find friendship and could be themselves.

The Community's life and worship together was another important tool in witnessing to the students. Even if they did not realise it before they arrived, no student was left in any doubt that it was a group of Christians who ran Lee Abbey. The chapel demonstrated this.

The first chapel had been a room on the ground floor of Melbourne, but when Courtfield came into use it was transferred to a small room leading off the main lounge, which had been the bridge room of the Overseas Visitors Club. At once there came a request that a door should be fixed to prevent the noise from the lounge disturbing the services. Gordon and Sheila felt very strongly that this should not be so. The worship of the Community was not to be a hidden activity, but open to any who might wish to come. Few students did so at first, but the influence was considerable and during evening prayers a number of residents would come and sit near the entrance, apparently reading newspapers, but clearly listening to all that was happening!

A real affinity was experienced between those who were believers. The great divide was not so much between the Christians and the rest, as between those who were people of faith, be it Christian, Hindu or Moslem, and those who had abandoned their original belief in their attempts to assert their identity or break away from their past. In the face of atheistic opposition, perhaps from a Marxist, the Christian and Muslim would find themselves standing together and even actively identifying with each other, the Muslim coming to prayers or the Christian observing

Ramadan. As anywhere, sorrow and joy drew people together. A young Jamaican law student died under anaesthetic when in hospital for a minor operation, and that evening half the Club packed into the chapel to mourn and listen to the Scriptures. On another occasion different religions were drawn together in worship to share the joy of a couple who were married in the chapel.

Although anybody was welcome to join the Community at prayers, it was always made clear that this was Christian worship. The evangelistic power of the Eucharist was demonstrated in a remarkable way at the second Christmas, when the Community were observing the midnight service as their corporate Communion. It was held in the Compass Room with an open invitation to the students. It was clearly explained that this was the celebration of the birth of Christ and to most people's surprise a large group of Ismaelis, some Hindus and a number of orthodox Muslims came to the service. However, they had not come merely to spectate. When the Christians came forward to receive the Sacrament, they came forward with them. For the Community it was a deeply moving experience, especially when afterwards several of them commented that it was the first time in their lives that they had experienced the presence of God. But a community does not only witness when it is worshipping. 'If you have love for one another then everyone will know that you are my disciples,' Jesus told His disciples. They were very much 'on show' the whole time and the students were only too conscious of everything that went on. They saw a group of people seeking to love and care for each other, working out the Christian values of love, justice and forgiveness in everyday life. They were equally aware when things were not right, and would note how the Community coped with personality clashes, grudges and petty jealousies.

The third area of witness was the witness of the spoken word. 'Why are you here?' 'Why work for so little money?' students might ask. Some would be curious, others mildly mocking. There was rarely an epilogue to verbalise the Gospel; it was up to the Community members to give a reason for 'the hope that was within them'. If they wanted to share what they believed, then they quickly learned that they had to be prepared to listen and learn from others before they could expect a hearing. It was not easy for a young Community member, often with no knowledge of other religions, to find himself in debate perhaps with a student studying for a Ph.D. who was intellectually superior and determined to argue.

As the mission of the Club began to be worked out in practice, it became clear that Christians of considerable spiritual maturity would be required if this work was to be done properly. At almost every meeting of the Council the Warden's report referred to the difficulty in finding Community members who were prepared to stay for a couple of years. This problem was not peculiar to the Club. In Devon Madeleine was finding similar difficulty in recruiting suitable girls, and in the wider Church, numbers offering for ordination were down, as were applications to the missionary societies. It was a feature of the sixties. In Gordon and Sheila, together with several other long-term members, the Community enjoyed strong leadership, but the continually changing membership and the shortage of staff was a constant strain. The Lee Abbey Community was not a place for those who were seeking a secure role; the relationship between Community and students could not be easily defined.

The pattern and structure of Community life in Devon had evolved over many years to fit the task and the circumstances; the same had to happen in London. Fairly soon the Community realised that they could have Associate members, a number of Christians with outside jobs such as college lecturers who would live at the Club, some acting as house wardens and some as unofficial tutors, and share in the pastoral work among students in the evenings and at weekends. Then there were students like Shoukry, an

Egyptian working on cancer research. A mature Christian, he exercised a valuable ministry among Community members and students alike with a particular gift of being able to bring together Christians and Muslims. The Christian ministry of the Club was not solely the prerogative of the Community. There were students who were older, both in years and spiritual maturity, than many Community members, and who were much more capable of relating to their fellow students.

Other assumptions that had been made at the beginning had to be questioned in the light of experience. Was it essential that the Community should personally undertake all the domestic work? Was it because so much of the work was dull and tiring that there was difficulty in recruiting Community members? Although this was the system used in Lynton, might it be more practical to employ outsiders to do much of the routine work, and have a smaller Community who could concentrate on relating directly to students? For a time outside contractors were brought in to take over the catering but this did not prove successful.

From all this, one thing which became clear was that the identity of the Community was much more difficult to establish in London than in Devon. The character of the Club was created by the presence of all who lived there, students and Community members alike. The Community saw that their attitude in the early days had tended to be paternalistic, wanting to do things for students – in reality their role was to take part with the students in the life of a wider community. For some this absence of a clear-cut identity was frightening, but for others it was exciting, for it reflected the work of Christ in the world, creating a community of love and justice among men of different races, faiths, cultures and political beliefs. 'It is the community of the Kingdom of God that we seek to make real. Our Club has to be a microcosm of that Kingdom . . .' wrote Denis Wakeling, Chairman of the Executive Committee.

By the time Chris Hayward succeeded Gordon as Warden in 1971, the Club was increasingly reflecting the full diversity of the student world. Initially it was assumed that the majority of the students would be doing postgraduate and undergraduate courses at the colleges in West London, and especially Imperial College, which is close to Earls Court. As time went on an incredible variety of students were staying at the Club. 'From forty different countries, doing forty different courses, at forty different colleges,' was the reply normally given to those enquiring about the sort of students who lived at the Lee Abbey Club. The courses ranged from hairdressing to hotel management, from architecture to aeronautical engineering; there were those doing postgraduate research, and those spending a year in London learning basic English at a private language school.

The changing economic situation also produced a notable variation in the countries from which students came. The number from African countries like Nigeria, who had been prominent at the beginning, began to decrease, while the proportion of Asians and those from the wealthy Middle East countries increased. The British Council's clause that the Club should take an agreed percentage of Commonwealth students became irrelevant in the light of actual requests for accommodation. This trend was to become even more noticeable in the seventies. During their times as Warden both David Johnston and Derek Barnes had to face the consequences of cut-backs in Government aid, the difficulty in obtaining visas, and the rapid increase of universities and colleges throughout the world. It was increasingly students from the wealthy countries who were coming to study in England. They brought with them the problems of affluence rather than poverty, needing to learn how to cope with responsibility and not to grasp at privilege.

The physical needs of students were also changing. In 1968 a further property, Sedan House, was purchased to provide bed-sitter accommodation to meet the increasing demand for accommodation for married couples. This raised major questions for the Community, as the needs of the students were now very different from those for which the Club had been set up.

As the students completed their courses and returned home so the true significance of the ministry of the Lee Abbey Club became apparent. Many were the intellectual elite of their society and returned to positions of great responsibility and influence. Some of those who had lived at the Club became Government ministers or took up senior posts in the legal and medical professions, the Civil Service and industry. The vast majority had not made any commitment to Christ, and had possibly not even expressed any interest in the Christian faith – the Club had merely been a convenient place to stay – but for two years they had been with a Christian Community, witnessing their life and the presence of the Holy Spirit whose work is not limited to the Church. There is no knowing what seeds were sown or what fruit will emerge in the years ahead.

The work of Lee Abbey in London was clearly established, but it was not easy to relate it to the work in Devon. When it was set up many people had assumed that it would be similar to Scargill in its relationship to the Devon Community, but the Council decided that they should be seen as one Community operating in two different ways. Devon and London were 'two expressions of the same concept' with the same basis of membership but independent in organisation.

There were natural links between them. Each found real encouragement in knowing that every morning Community members were praying for each other using the monthly prayer diary. Exchanges were arranged so that members of different departments experienced each other's work at first hand. It was good for the Club to be able to take groups of students down to Devon to see Lee Abbey and to enjoy the Devon countryside. For some people, this relationship was more than just a means of mutual encouragement; the existence of the London part of the Community was evidence of Lee Abbey working out its original vision more fully. The two parts needed each other. The Club needed the experience, financial backing and reputation of the Devon establishment, while Lee Abbey, which was sometimes accused of being too comfortable and isolated, could point to the work in London as evidence of its 'front-line' involvement.

It was not easy for either Community to feel the closeness of the bond that they had in theory. One difficulty was that they did not know each other. At the beginning, all the London Community had served in Devon. However, as new members joined, many of whom had never visited Devon, it became increasingly difficult at both ends for people to put faces to the names on the prayer list. The joint Chapter meetings and the exchanges helped them to get to know each other but with a continual turnover of members this was far from easy. Initially the London Community had adopted the pattern of life developed in Devon, but this was altered to fit their ministry so that after a while the two groups were using different Community promises, a different scale of allowances and a different organisational structure. It was a natural development that caused them to be regarded as two separate Communities.

During one of the very first visits of a party from the Club to Devon, Madeleine was sitting next to one of the students at dinner. By way of conversation she asked him, 'Where do you come from?'

'Oh, I come from Lee Abbey,' he replied. 'Have you ever been there?'

It was very clear that the Lee Abbey Fellowship now embraced not one, but two very important and very different works of God.

# 14

# When the Wind Blows

'Swinging' might be the popular image of the sixties, but for the Church in England it was a deeply disturbing decade. Throughout society it was an age of questioning and searching. Authority was being challenged in a way that had not been experienced before and the Church was not to escape.

As Billy Graham had become a household name in the fifties, in the sixties, it was John Robinson, Bishop of Woolwich who attracted enormous publicity, mainly through his book *Honest to God* which was published in 1963. For the academic, John Robinson was saying little that had not already been expressed by the liberal German theologians, but for many ordinary English church people the whole situation was bewildering. It appeared that the foundations on which their faith was laid were being questioned by the Church itself – the existence of a personal God, the historical facts of the life of Jesus Christ, the authority of the Bible as the Word of God. For a number of Christians, this requirement to think out what had always been assumed was refreshing and strengthening; for many others it had exactly the opposite effect. Perhaps hardest hit by the whole radical theology debate was evangelism – the very validity of which was, for some, in question. The vast publicity given to the views of the radical theologians meant that many non-Christians were only too aware of the confusion being experienced within the Church, and would summarily dismiss a simple evangelistic approach appealing to the authority of the Bible and the work and life of Jesus. How should Lee Abbey respond?

There was no doubt in the minds of Geoffrey and Jack that this new theology was not the message that God had entrusted to Lee Abbey. Jack wrote in the Editorial of *Christian Witness* (a quarterly magazine on evangelism published by Lee Abbey) in September 1963,'It is a strange delusion that so anaemic a Gospel, emptied of its life blood, can be "the power of God unto salvation" for modern man. In an age of astounding miracles it is already outdated. In an age of tempestuous doubt it offers soundings of no sure anchorage. In an age of deep and widespread spiritual hunger it offers a stone for bread.'

It was not possible simply to ignore what was happening, and continue with the well-proved approach, just waiting for this phase to pass. Groups such as ordinands, sixth formers and students demanded that the issues were faced. Geoffrey's epilogue on Personal Relationships, for example, was no longer receiving unchallenged acceptance. The 'P.R.' talk, though the subject was really sexuality and boy–girl relationships, had become a regular feature of many houseparties, especially those involving young people. Now, the so-called 'new morality' and situational ethics, which made love rather than law the criterion for moral decision-making, meant that Geoffrey's traditional conservative approach would be openly questioned.

While Lee Abbey was having to face these issues, the Council again had the important task of finding God's choice of a man to be Warden. At the January meeting in 1964, Geoffrey announced that as he was soon to be sixty he felt it was time for him and Dora to move on. He had been offered a number of jobs, including several overseas bishoprics which he had declined, but he felt that it was now right to consider moving. The previous few years had not been easy, either within the Community or in the wider Church, and he felt that a younger man was needed to lead Lee Abbey. As with Roger de Pemberton's departure in

1950, many people were going to find it very strange to think of Lee Abbey without Geoffrey – the place was so much identified with him.

At the end of the houseparty season in October 1964 Geoffrey and Dora moved to take up the post of Canon Missioner in the Coventry Diocese. It was a memorable departure. On their last day at Lee Abbey it was already dusk by the time they were finally ready to go. There was hardly anybody around as they said farewell to Madeleine in the yard and quietly slipped away. Then as their car turned out of the entrance tower they saw that the road to the Valley of the Rocks was lined by Community members carrying torches. As the car passed, each person followed it until the whole Community was gathered at the head of the Valley of Rocks. They had no doubt that they were marking the end of an era.

It is not easy to find the right person to follow a man who has been successful and popular. Geoffrey had clearly been God's man for Lee Abbey in the fifties, and now different qualities were needed in the man who could work out the vision in the sixties. Change would be essential, if Lee Abbey were to continue to speak to the Church.

The man chosen was Ken Pillar, vicar of St. Mary Bredin, Canterbury. For the Council, Ken's appointment had one great advantage; he had served as Chaplain at Lee Abbey for five years under Geoffrey. They were looking for change, not merely a continuation of Geoffrey's ministry, and in Ken they were confident that he would know what he was changing.

Ken's links with Lee Abbey went right back to the first houseparty season. While on leave from the Navy he had been intrigued to read of the new venture in North Devon and so had come to a houseparty. He was deeply impressed by all that he experienced that week and became a regular visitor, first as a student from Cambridge bringing friends to working parties, and then as a curate from Liverpool. When it was decided to appoint a Junior Chaplain he had been an obvious choice. So after an absence of seven years Ken and Margaret, with their four young children, moved back to Lee Abbey; on January 25th 1965, he was installed as the third Warden.

As expected, the Community soon discovered that Ken's style of leadership was very different from Geoffrey's. They had lost a father and gained an elder brother. Ken knew that he was not the omni-competent leader to which the Community had become accustomed. For some people, especially those who had been on the Community for a number of years, it was going to take time to adjust to a very different way of working which included much more delegated responsibility.

There was a significant relaxation of Community discipline. For example, the weekly corporate Communion service was put back half an hour to begin at six-thirty a.m. Rules that forbade men to visit the girls' rooms were lifted, and a very thorny issue was finally resolved when it was decided that tennis and putting could be played on Sundays, a question that had been debated at great length by the Council.

What was happening at Lee Abbey was no different from what was occurring in universities, colleges and similar institutions throughout the country – a swing towards greater freedom, more general involvement in decision-making and away from strict discipline.

Ken also brought a new theological approach to the ministry at Lee Abbey. Like Geoffrey he was a convinced evangelical, insisting on the need for personal conversion and commitment to Christ, yet he was noticeably more liberal in his approach. Although he would disagree with much of what the radical theologians like John Robinson were saying, he was anxious that they should not be dismissed out of hand. People needed to listen carefully to what they were trying to say before passing judgment. Greater openness became a feature of the houseparty programmes. Guests were encouraged to learn from each other in small discussion groups. Epilogues became shorter, covering a greater variety of subjects than the clear-cut pattern of the fifties which had looked in turn at God, Man, Sin and the Cross, leading to the challenge evening. Speakers would talk openly about doubts and uncertainties as well as convictions. It was inevitable that some guests, familiar with Lee Abbey under Geoffrey Rogers, would find the changes disturbing.

> One could not avoid the realisation of some of the currents flowing within the Community, [wrote a correspondent to *the Church of England Newspaper* about a recent visit to Lee Abbey] and I have no reason to doubt the accuracy of reports from respected Christian friends who went on other houseparties recently. They speak of Christians leaving in utter distress. What is the evangelistic impact of a place where the leading members of the Community seem unworried by the fact that they contradict each other openly upon matters of basic importance' . . . Some have always been dubious about Lee Abbey's attempt to make an appeal to all sections of the Church of England. I have always hoped that it would succeed, and I believe it still could. But it is a delicate tightrope to walk if a real evangelistic balance is to be maintained. [Referring to Cuthbert Bardsley's impending retirement from the Council:] one fears that his departure from the Chairmanship could be an omen of doom to this endeavour, which as you rightly say, has for twenty-two years been a tremendous influence for good in the Church of England.

This theological tension came to a head in the student working parties. For almost twenty years the Oxford and Cambridge University pastorates had been bringing groups of students together to the spring working parties. The two pastorates are very different in structure and organisation, and in the sixties they represented two distinct theological positions and approaches to evangelism.

The Oxford pastorate, based at St. Aldate's Church, was traditional in approach, seeing its task as evangelism and the nurturing of young Christians. The Cambridge pastorate was much more loosely structured, involving a number of college chaplains and including a radical element, with a strong intellectual emphasis.

As the two groups came together each spring the Community witnessed in microcosm what was happening in the Church. The main point of friction was the content of the evening epilogues by the pastorate Chaplains. Each side was deeply disturbed by the approach of the other. While the sympathies of the majority of the Community were probably with Oxford, the Chapter was anxious to remain impartial, believing that it was good for the groups to come together. They sensed that in the daily team meetings they were witnessing not merely a difference in theology, albeit a major one, but a failure in communication, with neither side listening to the other. In 1968 the two groups decided that it would be better if they came to separate working parties. It was a solution to a long-standing tension but it was accepted by the Community with great sadness. The one consolation was that both groups were still willing to maintain their links with Lee Abbey.

This whole dispute was very much a product of its time. In later years the situation was to be completely different, the two pastorates continuing to come on separate weeks but with a deep spiritual bond developing between them through Oxford staff and students sharing in the Cambridge week.

Nevertheless, the initial vision and challenge of Lee Abbey was not to be submerged by all this theological controversy; 1966 witnessed a great Lee Abbey gathering in London to celebrate the twenty-first anniversary. Cuthbert Bardsley reiterated the convictions on which Lee Abbey was founded as he preached at a Eucharist at St. Martin-in-the-Fields.

'This could be a dangerous moment, if we were merely to

rest content with the point that we have reached. What is God saying to us of Lee Abbey today? I believe that God is saying *first*, that nothing less than a major reformation is needed in Britain today, and *second*, if that is to happen, the Church must get her priorities right, and evangelism must be restored to its rightful place in the scale of the Church's values. And *third*, if that is to happen, we must be far more deeply converted than most of us are at this moment. And *fourth*, if that is to happen, we must be brought once again, face to face with a living, loving, saving Lord – the Lord of Calvary.'

In the afternoon the strength of the Lee Abbey movement was demonstrated when over 6,000 people filled the Royal Albert Hall for the rally, which included a testimony and two songs from Cliff Richard, whose recent conversion was still headline news. The theme was 'Time to Build . . . Time to Serve . . . Time to Act', and Donald Coggan, Archbishop of York, threw down the challenge of Christian service to young people.

The Community had hoped for a far greater response to this challenge than the subsequent letters indicated, but the whole day proved that there was no question that Lee Abbey was still sounding the same trumpet.

It was not only changes in the presentation of the Gospel and in theological thinking that guests began to notice during the sixties. The place was becoming more comfortable. This was the decade of affluence. Harold Macmillan had told the country that 'they had never had it so good', and materially he was right. The generally improved standard of living meant that guests could no longer be expected to put up with the relatively spartan conditions of the early years. If Lee Abbey were to attract holiday visitors, then it must offer the standard of accommodation and service found in private hotels. No longer were guests asked to bring their own sheets, and the purchase of a new washing-up machine meant that it was possible to dispense with the need for guests to take their turn at the sinks.

These improvements were a mixed blessing, for although it greatly added to the comfort of a holiday at Lee Abbey, guests and Community were no longer working together as before. A clearer distinction was emerging which saw the Community as those who served, and the guests as those who were being served.

Holiday visitors were also becoming accustomed to higher standards of accommodation. People were less willing to share rooms and Lee Abbey had only two single bedrooms, so it was decided to mark the anniversary by building a block of twelve new single rooms.

While the builders were at work on this new bedroom block the Community maintenance team were tackling the largest job they had ever faced – the rewiring of virtually the whole house. The increased load and general changeover from DC to AC meant that Lee Abbey could no longer rely on its diesel generators for electricity; the best solution was to convert to the mains supply. The working parties dug a four-foot trench from the horizon down to the main house, and for nearly a year a team of three Community members, only one an experienced electrician, set about rewiring much of the house to comply with the Electricity Board standards. It was a test for the whole Community. For months it seemed that the place was in chaos, with the builders outside and the rewiring inside, which in turn meant that many rooms also had to be replastered and decorated. Above all it was a race against time, for the changeover to the mains was needed at the same time as the new building came into use. Just in time for the Christmas houseparty the work was successfully completed.

As the improvements in facilities were making life more comfortable for the guests, for the Community they presented a new dilemma. Community membership no longer involved the material and physical sacrifice of the early days. Allowances were not large but with full board and keep provided, Lee Abbey offered a very secure job. There was no longer any question that there would not be sufficient money at the end of the week for allowances to be paid. Accommodation was cramped, but central heating meant that for many they were far warmer than they would have been at home. Machines like floor polishers and dish-washers meant that much of the work was no longer so hard. A number of people felt that there was a danger that Community life could become a soft option rather than the challenge that it had been before. Real disquiet was expressed at the news that the corridors were going to be carpeted. This decision was seen as symbolic that the pioneering days were over; the house would be much quieter and easier to clean, but for many Lee Abbey was becoming more like a hotel than the home of a Christian Community.

In practice, although Community life was more relaxed both physically and in terms of discipline, the result was not a great influx of Community members. In the second half of the sixties it was more difficult to find suitable applicants than at any time since 1945. Perhaps Community membership did not offer the excitement that many young people were looking for, and the general mood of the Church and society militated against this form of 'institutional service'.

Yet as life was getting easier, Community members were also given greater responsibility. One of the Community promises reads, 'Are you ready to serve, in every way, those who come to us, seeking to help one another to a clearer and deeper knowledge of Christ, through your work and by your words?' It has always been understood that all Community members have come to Lee Abbey to serve the Lord, and this service is equally worked out in cleaning lavatories or typing letters as in giving epilogues or counselling a person in need. There is great truth in the statement that 'No task is too humble for a Christian.' An important lesson which has to be learned in Community life is that each person needs to be clear and secure in his role, without jealousy of other people's tasks and responsibilities.

Community members, whatever their task, have always been expected to befriend guests and be prepared to be used by God to listen and to witness. Departmental duties meant that in practice this contact with the guests was restricted to meal-times and evenings. The general responsibility for the houseparty programme and pastoral work lay with the Chaplains and other senior members and about half a dozen of the guests, who each week were invited to join the houseparty team.

Changes began to be made which enabled much greater involvement of the whole Community in the direct ministry to guests. At first it was decided that one red-label member from each department should be chosen each week to join the houseparty team, to attend the morning team meeting and report back to his department on matters that needed specific prayer. It was then seen that as part of their training it would be good to involve Community members in planning programmes, attending sessions, leading walks and various activities.

These changes enabled a structure to develop which recognised that pastoral work belonged to the whole Community and allowed gifts to be discovered and more fully used. This involvement has continued to increase steadily so that Community members are now released full-time from departmental duties throughout their week on the team, to share in all the guest activities.

During the sixties Lee Abbey seemed to be walking through a minefield. Advance meant that risks had to be taken; wrong moves were made and explosions were set off. Yet the Community was very much alive, if a bit battered, when it came to the seventies – because in the middle of the battle, God Himself was doing a new thing.

# 15

# A New Thing

'I am asking for an openness to new ideas, a willingness to experiment which will not stifle the Holy Spirit if, as I believe he does, He wishes to do new things in new ways in a new age.'

Donald Coggan was preaching the sermon at the 1964 Reunion Service in St. Paul's Cathedral. Few people could have realised how prophetic his words were as he continued, 'This means that, if we give the Holy Spirit a chance, He will make Jesus so real to us that we shall see Him not as a figure of ancient history, but as our great Contemporary; and the results are not likely to be less disturbing than they were nineteen centuries back.'

Disturbing was the right word to describe the impact on the Church of the work of God, which was to bring renewed prominence to the person and work of the Holy Spirit. As books like *The Cross and the Switchblade* and *They Speak with Other Tongues* became popular, so the charismatic movement was the great subject of discussion at Christian gatherings, with those passionately in favour, those definitely against and many who were genuinely questioning and seeking. In its response to the charismatic movement Lee Abbey was to mirror what was happening in the wider Church.

The first recognition of the impact of the movement on Lee Abbey was recorded by Geoffrey in his final report to the Council as Warden in October 1964. After noting that the power of the Holy Spirit had been increasingly at work

during the summer season he wrote, 'The particular mani-
festation of private glossalalia has appeared, sought and
unsought among members of the Community and more
than a dozen members (almost, but not entirely all women
members) are now speaking with tongues in their own
private devotions.'

Geoffrey's initial reaction to the emergence of a group
within the Community who were speaking in tongues was
one of caution. He had only recently heard news from a
parish with which Lee Abbey had had close links over many
years, of a deep split in the congregation over this issue; it
was one of the first Anglican parishes in England to experience this new movement of the Holy Spirit. Some bad
mistakes had been made in the initial enthusiasm. Geoffrey
was most anxious that no similar division should be allowed
to arise within the Community and so weaken its evangelistic impact. He also realised that Lee Abbey was in a
position of considerable influence in the Church of England, and many people would be looking to the Community
for guidance and would take a lead from their response to
the charismatic movement.

A guarded editorial on the subject was published in
*Christian Witness*. It welcomed the reappearance of speaking in tongues within the Church and recognised that 'It can
be a means of wonderful spiritual uplift and blessing to the
receiver, and often a new beginning of Spirit-led life and
experience,' but followed this with a clear warning.

What those who have received the gift need to guard
against is the spiritual pride which supposes that because
of it they are higher in God's favour than those who have
not received it, or that they alone have received the
Baptism of the Holy Spirit and are Christians in the full
sense. It is this attitude which can easily cause and has at
times caused divisions among the brethren and the
destruction of Christian fellowship.

It was not long before there were several of the Community who had had some kind of charismatic experience, which usually involved speaking in tongues. Some had been seeking it in prayer like Stella. Before she joined the Community she had had a deep experience of God's love and power when confronted with her own failure to help a Christian friend in need. Feeling perplexed and utterly useless she knelt down before the altar rail in the small chapel adjoining the house where she was working.

'Oh God,' I thought hopelessly. Suddenly I was aware of the most tremendous sensation of love and peace flowing down through me until I was veritably tingling; with deep awe I knew the presence of God. I knew that He was with me, that He did care, that He even desired to use me in the extension of His glorious Kingdom. I cannot begin to describe the emotion of the moment only that I cried with joy that He should come to one such as me and that with all my heart, soul and strength I committed myself to Him in a way that had never before been possible. [Later that evening in her prayer time she found herself speaking in tongues.] What was this experience? The result of relaxation of high tension; the product of deep emotion? I can only say it is something that has revolutionised my life; for this spirit of awareness, this indwelling peace and great joy has been with me ever since.

For other people the experience came in unexpected ways; one girl was lying in her bath. The leader of the garden team was sitting at the back of the octagonal lounge praying for Geoffrey as he gave the epilogue when he realised that he was praying in an unknown language.

Some of them felt that the leaders did not share their enthusiasm and were being over-cautious in their approach. Geoffrey ruled that there should be no exclusive meetings for the exercise of the spiritual gifts and chapters twelve to fourteen of 1 Corinthians were used at the Community prayers to study the use and abuse of spiritual gifts. A similar approach was taken by Ken when he became Warden; there was to be no use of tongues in public, although private meetings could be held provided that they were open to any who wished to come.

There was no official Lee Abbey policy on the movement, because no such policy was possible. The Community, and especially the Chapter, contained those to whom their 'Baptism in the Spirit' experience had revolutionised their Christian lives, those who could testify to such an experience in the past but for whom it was less significant, and those who could claim no such experience. The challenge that the charismatic movement presented to Lee Abbey was whether such a mixed group could openly live, work and pray together, fully accepting one another in Christ and recognising that each had a continual need of the Spirit's touch. As Lee Abbey had always insisted on the necessity for personal conversion, so it had always claimed the necessity for Christians to be continually open to and filled by the Holy Spirit. In this work God was not limited to certain experiences or ways of working. The leaders of the Community believed that Lee Abbey needed to include those who came with different experiences of God and so of the Holy Spirit. In the early days of the charismatic movement in England this was a very difficult position to maintain. It produced tensions, for the devil delights to sow seeds of jealousy and spiritual pride to destroy the unity that Christ came to bring. At Lee Abbey he had a good try but he did not succeed.

As with the issue of churchmanship, Lee Abbey appeared enigmatic concerning the charismatic movement. Guests would not hear talks from Community members about Baptism in the Spirit or seeking spiritual gifts, but Michael and Jeanne Harper were invited as guest speakers. Although guests were not told that they ought to be seeking a charismatic experience, those who came to Lee Abbey conscious of their need of something new would often find God leading them to a Community member or a fellow guest who would talk and pray with them.

Such was the case at the Families Houseparty in June 1963. A number of young couples who were hungry for more of the Holy Spirit in their lives met together with two of the Chaplains. Not really knowing what to do, they all prayed for each other in turn with laying on of hands, open to the Lord for whatever He might want to do. It was a hallowed time of prayer and a deep spirit of repentance fell on them when confession was made of failure and fresh consecration promised. The words of the hymn 'O breath of life come sweeping through us' were often sung on that houseparty, and for that group who met for prayer it marked the start of a new experience of the Holy Spirit 'sweeping through' them. John and Gay Perry were among the group and their ministry in Chorleywood was transformed as a result of that time. Indeed, God was preparing them to return eventually to Lee Abbey when John was appointed Warden some thirteen years later. A number of senior Community members who had received a spiritual gift would exercise it freely in their ministry, for example, quietly praying in tongues during a service of prayer with the laying on of hands. However, many guests from churches which had experienced a great movement of the Spirit were anxious that Lee Abbey should take a much more positive line in encouraging every Christian to seek a second blessing experience and to speak in tongues.

Equally, there were guests who were uneasy and unhappy about the movement. Following those who taught that spiritual gifts ceased at the end of the apostolic age, they were convinced that the charismatic movement was founded on emotion and was irrelevant to the Gospel; they were anxious about what they saw and heard at Lee Abbey. If a question about this was asked in an Open Forum they would generally be told that spiritual gifts were entirely Biblical and although some of what was being claimed was possibly the product of emotional excitement, there was clear evidence that this was the work of the Holy Spirit. Community members would testify to being blessed in different ways, to discovering a new desire to pray and a liberation in their prayer life, and to healing in body and spirit. The result could be seen in their lives, often in new effectiveness in evangelism.

As it became increasingly obvious that this was not merely a nine-day wonder but a new spiritual movement throughout the world-wide Church, the true significance of what God was doing became clear. The fundamental issue was not about spiritual experience but about renewal. The work of God is to renew continually the lives of individuals – a constant process of which conversion is but the beginning – and to renew the Church as the people of God, leading in turn to the renewal of society. The Holy Spirit was reminding the Church of truths that had largely been forgotten, in practice if not in theory. Lee Abbey continued to be cautious of any teaching that was over-emotional in emphasis and which too narrowly channelled Christian experience. It became obvious, however, that many of the truths the charismatic movement was propounding were what Lee Abbey had been seeking to demonstrate since 1945.

Teaching on the use and place of spiritual gifts in building up the Body of Christ, on healing, on lay ministry and on freedom in worship, did not seem as revolutionary at Lee Abbey as it did in many other places. The Community was a Body of Christ's people in which many of those things were already being worked out and it was ripe for new encouragement. The ministry of healing was one such area.

For many years this had been part of Lee Abbey's ministry, mainly under the guidance of Jack Winslow. It was perfectly normal to pray for those who were sick, together with the laying on of hands and sometimes with anointing with oil. This was regarded as no mere empty ceremony. There was a real expectation that results would be seen and there were many people who could testify to experiencing God's healing touch.

One example was a clergyman from Somerset who had diabetic retinitis. Garth had been diabetic for twenty-three years when his sight began to fail. A specialist told him that within three months he would be totally blind and advised him to learn braille immediately. Despite the specialist's warning he somehow felt that he was never going to be permanently blind and enlisted the help of several hundred friends to pray. As his sight rapidly worsened he came down to Lee Abbey for a holiday, during the course of which he asked Jack and Geoffrey if they would lay hands on him and anoint him with oil. One afternoon a small group met in the chapel to pray with him. There was no dramatic physical change and to begin with he was a little disappointed, but he received an assurance of peace and well-being such as he had never experienced before. God had taken over and everything was all right.

After about three weeks he said to his wife one morning, 'I think the haemorrhages have stopped,' and as soon as possible he went to the specialist, not telling him what had happened. After the usual examination the specialist said, 'I am glad to be able to tell you that the haemorrhages have ceased.' Garth then told him what had taken place at Lee Abbey. Although the doctor was a Christian he was cautious, assuring him that although the bleeding had stopped this did not mean that there would be any recovery of sight as the damage to both eyes was great. He might retain a small measure of what is called 'location sight' provided there was no return of the haemorrhages. However, within three months he was able to read large print with a bright light and a powerful lens; within about six months he could read normally with ordinary spectacles. Within a year he was again driving his car.

The specialist agreed that this was a miraculous recovery and commented, 'Humanly speaking your eyes were finished; I have never in all my experience seen eyes that were in the mess that yours were in even begin to recover. I wish to God I could see more of this among my patients.' There have been many such testimonies to healing down the years.

Because there was already this keen interest in the subject an American, Agnes Sanford, well known through her books such as *The Healing Light*, was invited as a guest speaker on several occasions, including a number of clergy recesses. With her teaching on the healing of the memories, she brought a whole new dimension to the subject. She came with first-hand experience of the charismatic movement in America and laid stress on the work of the Holy Spirit, informally introducing a number of people for the first time to the idea of 'Baptism in the Holy Spirit'.

As well as her public speaking she counselled and prayed with a number of people for healing and both guests and Community members were blessed through her ministry. Throughout she stressed the need to bring healing back into the centre of the Church's life and worship. Many of the clergy returned to establish a healing ministry in their parishes and for the Community a consequence of her visit was that renewed prominence was given to prayer with the laying on of hands at the corporate Communion. There would be very few weeks at Lee Abbey in which there was not a service of prayer for healing. But although Agnes's visit brought a renewed confidence in the power of God to heal, the Community also had to discover the much harder lesson that physical recovery is not automatically the will of God. There was one person for whom Agnes said that she felt it was not right to pray for recovery, whom God used to teach the Community most about His power to heal.

Lily Lloyd was a great character in the Community. She came from a humble home in Cambridge, where she had been converted at Holy Trinity Church. Though she had few educational advantages, she had a natural wit and intelligence and could confound the wisest academics with her simple and direct faith. She came to Lee Abbey as second cook and her lively sense of humour and fund of entertaining stories about her experiences in the A.T.S. 'on the gun site' made the kitchen a place of much laughter. Being short of stature she was provided with a stool on which to stand when stirring the various mixtures brewing on the big ranges of the old kitchen. There she would stand and hold forth, her ringing voice and laughter carrying up through the yard to the chapel windows. She was never afraid to speak out if she saw anything wrong, but she had a warm and loving personality; she spoiled the Community boys, especially the farm lads, and many were the late-night supper picnics she produced at silage and haymaking time. Sadly, however, she developed cancer and had to have a mastectomy. Her return to Community life coincided with the purchase of Lee Mouth Cottage.

The owner, Mrs Budd, whose father had been woodsman for Squire Bailey, had decided that she ought to give up her cottage and move into Lynton. As the cottage was situated in the middle of the estate, next to the camp field and the road to the beach, Lee Abbey was most anxious to buy this and Mrs Budd was quite happy to sell.

It seemed ideal, once the cottage had been modernised, that Lil should live there together with her friend Ursula, who ran the farm. She could continue the Devon cream tea business, for which Mrs Budd had established quite a reputation in the area. But within two years the cancer had reappeared and Lil was very ill. Groups of the Community would gather round her bed to pray with her; there was real confidence that God would want to heal Lil and restore her to full health. It seemed natural when Agnes Sanford next visited to ask her to pray for Lil, and a real improvement was expected. Agnes taught, however, that before one prayed for healing it was essential to pray for guidance about God's will for the person, and she replied that she did not believe that it was God's will for her to pray for Lil's physical healing. It was hard to accept and understand. A couple of weeks later another guest, with wide experience in the healing ministry, was asked if she would pray for Lil. She laid hands on her claiming Christ's healing power, but Lil's physical decline continued and six months later she died.

Lil's illness and death were to have a profound effect upon the Community, bringing new depths of understanding about the power of the Holy Spirit and the ways of God. If there was a guest who seemed very preoccupied with their own problems it was often suggested that they might go down to the cottage to cheer up Lil. They would return astonished at her serenity and testimony to the love of God. God had given Lil the very special gift of being able to speak about her faith without any embarrassment.

The beautiful garden at the cottage which was created by landscaping a corner of the neighbouring field now stands as a permanent memorial to Lil. It is a picture of the work of God, the Holy Spirit, who transforms ordinary, rough lives to bring beauty, joy and peace.

# 16

## *Faith in the Field*

'I can't stand it here!' moaned a young girl. 'I've never been surrounded by so much love, I want to go home.'

It was five p.m. on a Saturday afternoon. An hour before, she had arrived at the Lee Abbey Youth Camp, been given a name badge, allocated to a tent and handed a plastic mug of rather indifferent tea! Not a word had been spoken to her about the Christian faith, but she could sense that the place was totally foreign to her experience. Later she was grateful that she had been persuaded to stay.

Each August the field below the house overlooking the bay is the setting for two summer camps. Each lasts a fortnight and takes about 120 young campers aged between sixteen and twenty-five, cared for by a team of thirty volunteer workers. The age group is one of the main reasons why camp has had as great a spiritual impact as any other aspect of Lee Abbey's work. On this truly sacred ground many have met with the living God and had all their adult life changed as a result.

Crockpits – the headland beyond Lee Bay – was the site of a small camp in 1947, but the first camp organised on the present field was in 1948. Far less exposed, it has proved ideal: it slopes down towards the sea, drains quickly and is protected from the prevailing south-westerly wind by the hillside. Only when the wind is from the north-west, a fairly rare event, does everybody have to be prepared to hold down the tents!

The first Commandant, as the leader of the camp used to be styled, was Arthur Westall, a schoolmaster who had become a Christian at Lee Abbey the previous summer. He and his wife were wondering where to go on holiday when she noticed an advertisement for Lee Abbey in a newspaper used to wrap up some fish.

'Here is the place for us, nice and cheap and grand country.' He looked at it.

'Not for me,' he said, 'Church of England Centre! They will want to shove religion down our throats there.' But his wife got her way, and they came. Although he was the headmaster of a Church School, and a church warden, he had lost his Christian faith. During the holiday the friendliness he encountered melted his suspicions. The absence of 'buttonholing' put him at ease and he became intrigued by the spirit of the place. The fresh presentation of the old truth brought a return of faith and he sought out one of the speakers and with his help renewed his commitment to Christ. He went back to his work with a new vision and new zest, and his staff and pupils alike were conscious of the change. The next year God was using Arthur's new-found faith as a powerful instrument in establishing the Youth Camp.

For the first two years the camp was distinctly makeshift in its organisation. There were virtually no special facilities on the field itself other than the large marquee used for eating and meetings, and the latrines. Nearby streams were used for washing, the cooks alone being allowed the privilege of going up to the main house for baths. Bell tents were hired from the Army. For both cooking and hot water they relied on a couple of open-air field kitchens, which were very difficult to use, especially in the rain.

This was all changed when Raymond Scantlebury, always referred to as 'Scant', took over as Commandant in 1950. Under his leadership the whole thing was put on a much more organised footing, with ridge tents for sleeping and a fire shelter to ease the cook's task.

Scant's influence on the camp was enormous and he determined the basic pattern of its life and ministry which has continued into the eighties. Infectious in his faith in Christ, he was a gifted evangelist. He had wanted to go to Africa as a missionary with C.M.S., but he was not physically strong and therefore not permitted to go overseas. Instead he was appointed as Canon Missioner in Carlisle Diocese, a post which offered plenty of scope for him to fulfil his calling to preach the Gospel.

Two particular qualities characterised his ministry. As a non-academic he could convey simple truths to intellectual people, and he possessed that rare gift of friendliness that was able to convince everyone to whom he spoke that he really cared and loved them. But above all he encouraged high expectations of God. It was the charismatic approach in the days before the charismatic movement. He believed that God was going to work miracles and people were going to be converted and that was why God had brought them to the camp. Each year saw his faith vindicated.

This was not high-pressure evangelism; indeed his approach was the exact opposite. A camper who wished to talk to Scant had to seek him out and he would not make it easy. As often as not a person who came to Scant and asked to talk about a problem would be met with, 'Now I shall be busy for the next twenty minutes, would you do something for me, just go over to the chapel tent and put your problem to Jesus, just talk to Him about it. In about half an hour I shall be free.' Some time later that day Scant would search the person out.

'By the way, you wanted to come and see me.'

'Oh, well, I don't need to now because while I was in the chapel tent . . .'

It was an approach which demonstrated that his confidence was in God and not in himself.

Scant's death in 1958, only a few months before he was to lead the camp for his ninth successive year, was a great loss to Lee Abbey. The mantle of leadership passed to Reg

Sanger who had been Scant's adjutant and he did the job for the next two years.

With two outside houseparties as well as a full house, August was the busiest time of the year for the Community. For this reason the camp has always been organised separately from the work of the main house. For the next few years, however, leadership was taken over by the Chaplains, John Collie in 1960 and then Michael Vickers. When it was time for Michael to leave, there was no obvious person at Lee Abbey to take over. The question of the leadership became a matter for much prayer until one afternoon Ray Fardon, a member of the camp team for many years under Scant, came over to visit Lee Abbey from the outside houseparty at St. Audries. He talked with Michael and the result was that a few days later he received an invitation to take over the leadership of the camp. Although accepting 'for a year until one of the Chaplains is free to take it on again' he was to be the Commandant for the next twelve years.

Ray closely followed the approach that Scant had established. He held the deep conviction that every single person was brought to camp by God with a definite purpose. The team were to pray that God would not allow anyone to come whom He was not going to bless and Ray would encourage them to look for nothing less than one hundred per cent conversions from camps even when at times only one in ten of those coming were Christians. To the outsider this approach might seem naive and arrogant yet it was taken afresh each year, in the belief that camp was a very special work of God and that this was what God was challenging them to ask of Him.

Each year would see their prayers answered, and if they did not see every camper confessing faith in Christ during the fortnight, there was real thanksgiving in the knowledge that God was touching, in different ways, the lives of all who had been present. Since 1978, when Ray retired, the leadership has again been taken over by one of the Chaplains, Mike Battison. Having been first a camper and then a regular member of the team, he continues to lead very much in the tradition of Scant and Ray.

As Lee Abbey's ministry is that of the Community led by the Warden, so the camp's is that of the team led by the Commandant. The team has come to have a far more significant role than merely undertaking all the practical jobs. At the early camps it was a very haphazard process that brought the team together. There was usually a group of students from the London College of Divinity, but otherwise it was a matter of friends inviting friends. As everything became more organised under Scant so people were selected in advance and a preparatory weekend was introduced. It was held around Easter and enabled the team to get to know each other, to do advance planning and to pray together.

Although the team is only together for a maximum of four weeks each year a close fellowship has developed. One reason is that the majority of members, who may previously have been campers, stay on the team for three or four years and so in any year at least two-thirds will have served together before. Other informal meetings such as reunions and weddings maintain links throughout the year. The spiritual bond between them is experienced in different ways. An example of this was seen during the sixties when the team included Mike, a young Army officer in the Parachute regiment. It was during the troubles in Cyprus and at the last minute he was prevented from coming to the preparation weekend. During the Communion service on the Sunday morning four team members in turn felt compelled to pray for Mike though no one was clear why.

The next morning the reason came clear when Mike's picture was on the front page of the *Daily Express*. It was illustrating an article describing an incident that had taken place on the previous morning, the very time at which they had been praying. He had walked into an Eoka-held village, where four of his men were being held captive. With guns trained on him he had gone up to the Eoka leader and led his men out to safety. Later he described how, at that moment, he was suddenly very conscious of being uplifted by prayer.

This bond within the team is the foundation of the camp's Christian witness. Each tent is led by a team member whose responsibility is both the practical and spiritual welfare of those campers. At the heart of camp is the daily team meeting before lunch which can last for anything up to two hours! Here they worship together, plan the next day's programme and pray in depth for each member of the camp. Experience has taught that until the team is truly united then spiritual progress on camp is slow.

Shifting social patterns mean that there have been changes over the years among those who come as campers. Initially a camp was advertised for sixteen- to thirty-year-olds but the upper limit was soon lowered to twenty-five. In the fifties it was usually a very mature group with the average age over twenty. With the ending of National Service, the camp became younger, the majority being teenagers. Later another major change was noticed: after many years of camps where most were non-Christians, it was clear that now many of those coming had already made some form of commitment to Christ. This was a consequence of the general spiritual awakening taking place among young people, often through charismatic renewal. In addition to their primary work of evangelism, the team had to include training for those who had had an experience of the reality of Christ but whose roots were often very shallow and who needed to relate their experience to the full challenge of the Gospel.

The realisation that God was calling them to strengthen the teaching emphasis of the camp made no difference to the form of the programme. One of the most surprising features of the camp to the outsider has always been the lack of organised meetings and activities – far fewer than at the main house. A member of the Post Green Community in Dorset, which runs a similar camp, commented after a visit, 'It is incredible. You only have a morning Bible study and an evening epilogue while we are filling the day with meetings, yet the final result is the same.' Each day there is a voluntary Bible study before breakfast in the chapel tent, and during the second week a teaching session after tea. Otherwise campers are free to do exactly as they wish, swim, laze in the sun, go on walks or have a cream tea at the cottage over the fence. The one time the whole camp is certain to be together is at the evening epilogue. Although this is not compulsory there is strong encouragement to attend. One of the few camp rules is that everybody must be present on the field by nine p.m. – the time when the epilogue begins.

During the sixties, while epilogues in the house were tending to get shorter, at camp they began to get longer and seldom lasted less than an hour, made up of worship and teaching. The well-established logical pattern which looked in turn at God, Man, Sin, Jesus, the Holy Spirit and the Christian life, continued to be followed even when it was no longer being used at the house. In content the epilogues have attempted increasingly to reflect the swiftly changing needs of young people in each generation. In the sixties the challenge of the so-called 'new morality' and the questioning of biblical truth and authority meant that a strong emphasis was placed on the importance and integrity of the Bible as God's unchanging Word.

In the mid-seventies the massive general interest in the occult, with the involvement of many young people, became a dominating issue. In personal counselling many campers required help and ministry because of their dabbling with ouija boards, spiritism and other occult practices, which at the time had appeared harmless but which resulted in a spiritual bondage. This necessitated careful teaching about spiritual warfare.

Towards the end of the seventies the frequent breakdown of relationships within the family was becoming a decisive influence in the experience of young people. The 'Personal Relationships' epilogue had always been of crucial importance, coming at the end of the first week of camp before the challenge evening. Now, with many campers coming from broken and divided homes, nearly all the opening epilogues are built around this subject, with emphasis on Christ's work in reconciliation, the need to forgive and accept forgiveness, and the power of the Holy Spirit to change lives and situations. This approach to the Gospel has been found to communicate to many young people and bring healing to their own family situations.

The rest of the programme has seen surprisingly few alterations and several events have become established traditions. For example, every year visitors to the estate witness the spectacle of the entire camp in fancy dress, marching up the toll road to challenge the houseparty to the game of Podex. Facing the common enemy is invaluable in uniting the camp, although victory is not a foregone conclusion! Camp sports are always included in the programme although there is now less emphasis on physical activity than there was in earlier days, especially when Michael Vickers was Commandant. His keen interest in the Outward Bound scheme led to 'Operation Enterprise'. Held on the middle Saturday it was a combination of initiative test and camp sports with the entire camp divided into teams for a whole variety of activities throughout the estate.

In the late 1950s a survey was conducted revealing that there were well over 200 people in full-time Christian ministry who claimed that the Lee Abbey Youth Camp had played a major part in their spiritual growth. There is no doubt that this number has continued to increase with every camp.

A major influence is the witness of the team working and praying together. For the camper there is also the experience of being with a group that is free to express itself without too authoritarian a check on behaviour. Within a well-structured and disciplined environment there is true freedom. Nevertheless, whatever the elements that account for the profound impact of this camp, in the end the decisive factor is that it is founded on the work of God rather than the techniques of man. This has been demonstrated many times. On several occasions campers have come up to a member of the team after the Communion service on the first Sunday morning full of joy with the news that they have just surrendered their lives to Christ. Here is God at work, for no challenge has been put to them other than the words and experience of the Communion service itself! The atmosphere of the camp has a profound effect. One boy from a very unhappy home reflected, 'What means so much to me about this camp is the peace in this place' – an extraordinary comment from someone living in close proximity to 150 lively young people.

The influence of camp is sometimes only fully realised years later. Charlie was one of a number of Teddy boys from the East End of London who had been persuaded to come to camp by his youth club leader. He would not go into the epilogues but was prepared to talk for hours. Suddenly, after about ten days, without any explanation he announced that he was going home. It was three years before any news was heard about what had happened to Charlie and then the reason became clear. Charlie had known that if he had stayed any longer he would have become a Christian. Before he came, however, the gang to which he belonged had made it clear that if he did that they would mark him for life with their razors and chains. He knew it was no idle threat. It had taken him two years to extract himself from the gang. The next news of Charlie was that he was church warden of a struggling East End parish!

God's control of all that happens at camp has never been more dramatically demonstrated than in 1971. Early on in the first camp Ray had invited a new team member, Dave, to give the epilogue on the Holy Spirit. It was the first time that he had ever spoken in public and he was extremely nervous. This, combined with the fact that he was naturally softly spoken and had a strong Liverpudlian accent, meant that he was going to find it difficult to make himself understood! As soon as he began to speak disaster struck, for it began to pour with rain, which thundered on the canvas of the marquee. Frantic signs from the back to speak up were of no avail; not even those sitting in the front row could hear a word of what he was saying!

As Dave finished speaking the rain stopped. His final sentence was the only one to be heard, 'If you feel that your Christian life is inadequate then come over to the chapel tent and we will pray about it.'

It appeared that the evening had been a fiasco. Why did God allow it to rain throughout the epilogue? Ray felt particularly despondent. Yet only a few minutes after the epilogue he heard some beautiful singing coming from the chapel tent. Picking his way across the field where the atmosphere was still heavy after the storm he came across a small circle of campers praying together and jumping up and down with joy. A little further on was another group, and in the chapel tent itself he found a large crowd singing together in tongues, praising God in the most glorious harmony. That evening can only be described as another Pentecost. In His sovereign power the Holy Spirit had descended upon the camp and touched many lives. The next day at the team meeting the camp's programme had to be hastily reorganised to provide suitable teaching for the large number of new Christians. Dave was asked to give the same epilogue during the second camp. He did, though it did not rain and the response was not repeated.

Only at the end of August did it become clear that the mighty blessing granted by God at that first camp was His preparation for a very difficult second camp. Before the camps began Ray had received a word from God: 'You are to stand back and let the young ones do the witnessing.' He assumed this referred to him as leader and that God wanted the younger team members to play a larger part in the ministry. Dave's epilogue seemed to confirm this. However, it was a prophecy for the whole team.

The camp was proving difficult because of a number of campers with complex spiritual problems. At the end of the first week, Simon, one of the campers, went missing. Normally the police would not be over-concerned at news of a missing teenager, but this was different: Simon was epileptic. The field was filled with police, coastguards, a TV crew and even the Army, and the routine of camp was abandoned as most of the team, together with older campers, became fully involved in the massive search operation. No sign was found until Thursday, when a track was discovered on the cliff edge near Hunters Inn, which indicated where he must have gone over the cliff. His body was never recovered.

Even in this tragedy, the hand of God was evident. Before he went missing Simon had acknowledged Jesus as Lord of his life. In the camp, with all the team out searching, the ministry was not allowed to suffer: with camper ministering to camper another mighty work of the Holy Spirit took place. It was deeply humbling to the team to see the fulfilment of the earlier word that 'the young ones do the witnessing'.

For some time now the culmination of every camp has been a Communion service on the final evening. After supper the marquee which has been dining room, meeting room, and as often as not a shelter from the rain, is transformed. The sides of the tent and the central poles are swathed in leaves and ferns. Three chandeliers of candles provide light and at one end all the paraffin lamps are lit and assembled on a table. An atmosphere of great beauty is created with the scent of the greenery, the flickering candle light and the glow of the pressure lamps. When everything is ready the campers are invited in. It is a breathtaking sight, a symbol for many of what the camp has come to mean to them – a green temple, a place for meeting with the living Christ.

During a straightforward Communion service, following the traditional Anglican pattern, there is an opportunity for anybody to come forward to receive a simple cardboard cross as a token of any step of faith taken during camp. This is an act of both will and emotion. Some do not wish to take a cross and are respected for that. However, there are many who do – a testimony to young lives touched by God.

As people greet one another and say farewell during the Peace, they acknowledge that during the fortnight God has made them into the Body of Christ. They go out to share in the wider body of the Church and of the world, which for many of them is going to be far from easy. For Lee Abbey there is deep thanksgiving that Christ has once again met with all those he has brought onto the field.

# 17

# Merely a Happy Hotel?

'Does the Gospel people hear at Lee Abbey make heavy enough demands on them? . . .

'Does it invite people to go on in prayer, not to struggle to recapture their first experience but to let God take them on to the further reaches of fellowship with Him.' . . .

'Does the Gospel proclaimed here at Lee Abbey invite people not to be content with easy answers to hard problems, but to love God with their minds? . . .

'Does the Gospel proclaimed here really invite people to take the world seriously as loved and redeemed by God, and as the only material for the making of His Kingdom? . . .

'Does the Gospel proclaimed here send people away basically fearful and defensive or does it send them away hopeful, liberated, ready to take initiative?'

Geoffrey Paul was giving his last Warden's charge to the Community. This is an annual occasion on the Tuesday in Holy Week, when at the corporate Communion the red-label Community members renew their promises and the Warden shares with the Community something of what he senses God is saying. Geoffrey returned to a theme that had been one of his constant concerns during his five years as Warden. It remained an underlying question for the Community throughout the seventies.

For a regular visitor to Lee Abbey this was a time when there was little outward change. Community members continued to come and go, with people like Ursula, Pat,

Edna and Audrey providing the links with the past. Improvements to the buildings meant that the general standard of comfort continued to rise. The major work was the construction of the new kitchen in the old inner courtyard. As with the rewiring this was carried out largely by the Community's own maintenance team and it not only improved the cooking facilities but also created a new coffee area, providing more space for guests to chat together after meals. Otherwise those who came to stay would remark how little the place had outwardly altered.

Letters continued to indicate the varied ways in which God was using Lee Abbey and blessing the ministry, yet there was an underlying sense of uncertainty within the Council and the Community. It was wrong to assume that just because the house was full with guests and they were being blessed, that therefore Lee Abbey was fulfilling its task.

Plenty of new people were coming, almost fifty per cent each year – but the majority were either committed Christians or those from a church background. Lee Abbey was no longer attracting people from outside church circles and although there were still many guests for whom the Gospel message was completely new, it was clear that the Community was not touching the unchurched masses. Some feared that the place was becoming just a very happy hotel providing spiritual refreshment for Christians, rather than an evangelistic centre.

This concern for the role of Lee Abbey influenced many of the major decisions that had to be made during this period; for example, the way that Lee Abbey reacted to the problem of inflation. The policy had always been to keep fees as low as possible, to enable the maximum number of people to afford to come. Suddenly massive increases were required. For a few years the fees were kept down, but as it was realised that inflation was not going to stop, an increase of forty-two per cent was needed to account for V.A.T. and to place the work once more on a sound financial footing.

Keeping pace with inflation meant that fees rose from £10.10*s* per week in 1970 to £64.00 per week by 1980. Inevitably there were people who could no longer afford to come, but the predicted drop in guest numbers did not take place. At the same time it became firm policy to increase bursaries so that financial aid was more freely available to help those often most in need of a break at Lee Abbey, who would otherwise be unable to afford the fees to come.

However, money was only one of the factors which determined who should come to stay. Even if the fees could be kept very low, many of those people whom the Community wished to reach would have found the whole environment of Lee Abbey totally alien to their way of life. There was no bar, grace was said before meals, the whole concept of a holiday houseparty was off-putting to many people. The question that faced the Community and the Council was whether Lee Abbey should accept that its ministry was limited, or should actively seek ways of reaching a wider group of people. One proposal to establish a camp site on the estate was explored, but the plans came to nothing when planning permission was not granted.

In the Lee Abbey structure the Warden is the key man in determining the nature of the Community's work. Two men, Geoffrey Paul and John Perry, held the post during the seventies and in making each appointment the Council were clearly seeking a man who would bring a fresh direction to the work.

Geoffrey Paul, Canon of Bristol Cathedral, replaced Ken Pillar, who moved in 1970 to become vicar of Waltham Abbey. Unlike Ken's appointment, six years before, which had been a closely guarded secret, this was far more open – even Friends were asked to send in names of people whom the Council might consider for the post.

Geoffrey had made a great impression on the Chapter in Devon when he had come as guest speaker for the International Houseparty in 1969. Before moving to Bristol, where he was responsible for ordinands and post-ordination training, he had served for fifteen years in South India, spending much of that time teaching in a theological college. With his wife, Pam, and their five daughters, Geoffrey moved to Devon in July 1971. As at Ken's arrival, the Community found that they had to adjust to a very different style of leadership. After a period during which decision-making had become increasingly a corporate responsibility, Geoffrey was very much a father figure both in leadership and as pastor and counsellor. To have as Warden a man who was at heart a theologian with a deep love of the Bible was a new and challenging experience. Ken had been anxious that guests should be encouraged to look outwards, away from a self-conscious personal religion to embrace the wider problems of society. Geoffrey, too, was concerned that Lee Abbey should be a place where people were challenged to consider their faith, and to return home to relate it both to their local church and to the world. Although healing and renewal continued to be a central part of Lee Abbey's ministry, he stressed that, as in the ministry of Jesus, there must be a balance between meeting people's needs with God's revealing power, and challenging people in their strength to go and change the world. He was also concerned about the attitude of the Community to those who came to stay. There was a danger of seeing every guest in terms of a problem, needing healing, counselling and propping up, rather than as a potential warrior for Christ, to be charged for a personal mission.

Geoffrey taught that the world should be taken seriously. As he wrote to the Friends, 'I suspect we too easily give encouragement to those who are afraid of, or a bit shocked by today's world, and do not do enough to encourage those who are fascinated by all the dangerous and wonderful power, ingenuity, imagination and inventiveness in every sphere of life that God has given to men, and who want to get in amongst it all to claim as His and for Him. Are the Christians who go out from here sufficiently up at the front of change, reform and development, social, economic and international?'

To provide stimulation, alongside the Community pastoral team Geoffrey invited a much greater diversity of guest speakers than had come to Lee Abbey in the past. It was a deliberate attempt to bring a wider intellectual content and challenge to the teaching. It was a controversial policy provoking strong reaction from a number of guests and Community members, especially from those who were disturbed whenever the Gospel was not presented in traditional evangelical terms.

Geoffrey was anxious that the Community should attract people from outside the usual church-going belt to consider the claims of Christ, but it was not easy. In 1972 three houseparties were set aside, nicknamed 'Wild Weeks', with the aim of breaking away from the traditional programme structure and presenting the Gospel in more contemporary language. In the newsletter, Friends were encouraged to bring along people who they knew would normally regard the idea of 'a religious holiday at a place like Lee Abbey' with horror. It was a bold idea but the response was very disappointing, for when the guests arrived it was clear that the majority were from Christian backgrounds and that links with the unchurched masses had not been made.

During the early seventies Lee Abbey was breaking new ground in its ministry to guests through the use of the creative arts. Spearheaded by the renewal movement throughout the Church, there was a re-emergence of the arts, music, drama, art and poetry, both as a means of communication and as an expression of worship.

At Lee Abbey this was experienced in a highly original and at times unconventional way through two Chaplains, Philip Humphreys and Doug Constable. Both were very gifted musicians and their approach sought to embrace the full range of musical traditions. Presentations became a regular feature of many houseparties, involving a large part of the Community; at times they were based on dramatic and musical material specially composed for the occasion. Themes as diverse as the plagues in Egypt, Job, and the history of the Lynton–Barnstaple railway were tackled. At Christmas the traditional Nativity tableau was replaced by a highly imaginative production. Guests, too, often found themselves caught up in a virtually spontaneous production which would be rehearsed and performed in the course of one evening. A 'Gospel and Arts' week became a regular addition to the houseparty programme. A whole new area of Christian expression was being opened up which challenged Community and guests to discover and use the full range of the arts in worship and evangelism – something that was happening throughout the Church – and also to be actively creative in composing and writing and painting.

At Lee Abbey this was a more controversial subject than in many other places. Inevitably there were those who needed to be convinced that it was right for Christians to be involved in the arts – the strongly cerebral approach of traditional Protestantism was still deeply entrenched. Doug's and Philip's style was also provocative in itself, for it challenged people to see Christian truth in a highly personal way, producing strong reactions from guests and Community, with some agreeing all the way, some shaking their heads in incomprehension, some almost shaking their fists in desperation; but they never failed to touch people at unexpected times and to open the way for further conversation and deeper commitment.

These positive attempts to bring in new guests and explore different methods of communication re-established Lee Abbey as a centre for evangelism. Yet it was an approach to evangelism that was very different from that of the founders. As the seventies progressed there were fewer and fewer links with the early days to remind the Community of the daring faith and vision which had been at its foundation.

Several events underlined this growing separation from the past. In 1974 Jack Winslow died. It was twelve years

since he had retired from Community life to live in
Godalming, but he had retained his passionate interest in
Lee Abbey. His death was absolutely in keeping with his life.
In March 1974, at the age of ninety-two, he decided to
revisit India, the scene of his early ministry. Within forty
hours of his arrival he found himself again preaching in
Marathi, with the old fluency returning even after so many
years. He revisited the Ashram at Poona which he had
founded in 1921 and discovered that after some years of
decline it was developing strongly again in an ecumenical
fellowship of the Spirit. The whole tour was one of great
joy, as he had reunions with old friends, their sons and
grandsons! A few days after his return to England Jack
went into hospital with symptoms of heart trouble; after
receiving Holy Communion with the local vicar he died
peacefully at the completion of a long and very fruitful life.

The next year saw the thirtieth anniversary of the
purchase of Lee Abbey, with celebrations to give thanks to
God for all that He had accomplished in Devon and
London. They underlined both how much the work had
developed, and also that it was now a different era for Lee
Abbey. As for previous reunions, a large gathering was
arranged in London with a Communion service at St. Paul's
Cathedral and a rally at the Royal Festival Hall. Over 1,400
people were present, but it was a mere shadow compared
with the days when St. Paul's had been packed to the doors,
and the Festival Hall appeared to be less than half full.
People no longer flocked to mass gatherings in the way that
they had in the fifties. For the first time the seven men who
had led the Community as Wardens, four in Devon and
three in London, were brought together. Beginning with
Roger de Pemberton they traced the development of the
work. Sitting alongside the seven clergymen on the plat-
form was one woman, Madeleine, who as Lady Warden in
Devon for twenty-eight years had served under each Warden in turn, providing continuity with the past. By the time
of the reunion she had already decided that she should

retire. Her departure severed another major link in the Community with the early days. Without her presence some further change of direction was inevitable.

It seemed that the Community was only beginning to adjust to the changes resulting from Madeleine's departure when once again there was to be a new man as Warden. After nearly six years at Lee Abbey Geoffrey Paul was appointed to be Bishop of Hull. As his successor the Council chose John Perry, a man who knew Lee Abbey well. He and his family had been coming as guests for over twenty years and on a number of occasions he was a guest speaker. John and Gay had decided to become engaged there and together they had received a rich blessing from the Holy Spirit while staying at Lee Abbey in 1963.

On July 20th, 1977, Geoffrey Rogers spoke of the enormous sense of expectancy in the air as Denis Wakeling, now Bishop of Southwell and Chairman of the Council, installed John as the fifth Warden and welcomed John and Gay with their five children to the Community.

There seemed to be little doubt in anybody's mind that the new Warden would bring big changes. As Geoffrey had been appointed to bring theological weight to the Community's ministry, John came from a parochial background. For the previous fifteen years he had been vicar of St. Andrew's, Chorleywood, which under his leadership had become well known as a parish greatly blessed through the renewal movement and which had developed an effective evangelistic strategy in its ministry.

A few years earlier it would have been unthinkable for anybody with known charismatic connections to be even considered for the post of Warden. The intention had always been that Lee Abbey should be seen as serving the whole Church, though in practice it was very doubtful if this had been achieved for a long time; a Warden identified with one particular party was not thought to be a good idea. John's appointment reflected not so much a major change of policy by the Council, but an indication of the way that the new work of the Holy Spirit was becoming recognised: not in the creation of a new 'charismatic sect' but in bringing renewed life to the mainstream churches. Those who assumed that under John's leadership, Lee Abbey would become an exclusively 'charismatic community' were to be wrong. John's vision was that Lee Abbey should continue to serve the whole Church. The basic concern remained the same – the continuing search to discover the real role that God wanted Lee Abbey to play as a centre for renewal and evangelism. Having valued Lee Abbey's ministry as a guest, and from his experience in Chorleywood, John had shared with the Council before his appointment two specific areas that he believed needed to be developed.

The first concerned the ministry to the guests who came to stay – the problem raised by the image of the 'happy hotel'. In Geoffrey's time the key word had been 'challenge', now it became 'encouragement'. In addition to the holiday houseparties where people could come away to relax and find renewal in body, mind and spirit, John believed that the whole area of training, both for clergy and laity, should be expanded. This was particularly true in the winter months when, apart from the Christmas period and at weekends, the house was little used.

For the first time in the winter of 1978–9 a conference programme was arranged, covering a whole range of topics and using both the Community and guest speakers. This first programme was most encouraging. Many conferences proved to be an immediate success such as those for clergy wives, on rural ministry and preparation for retirement. One or two (including 'The Family in Society') found little support and had to be cancelled. As an experiment several non-residential one-day conferences were mounted to cater specifically for the churches in the West Country – an area for which Lee Abbey was feeling an increasing burden. They were warmly received, and have become a part of the annual programme.

In an attempt to encourage increasing numbers to come to Lee Abbey, to both conferences and houseparties, attractive modern publicity was seen to be necessary. Slowly people are beginning to think of Lee Abbey as a place offering concerted training as well as being a Christian holiday centre.

John Perry's other priority was the expansion of the Community's outreach work. At Chorleywood he had experienced the evangelistic effectiveness of small teams of Christians going out from the church to share their faith and learn from other congregations. The Community contained ideal resources to be used in a similar way. While previously the Community had been involved in two ten-day missions each year, there is now a substantial outreach programme with small teams going out most weeks during the winter months involved in ten-day missions, parish training weekends and one-day events such as visits to schools, colleges, deanery synods and even agricultural shows. The policy has not been to create a specialist outreach team; the opportunity to go out is deliberately spread throughout the whole Community so that teams go not as highly trained experts, but as representatives of a group of Christians who live together and are able to share their differing gifts and insights.

Lee Abbey's diversity in Christian experience and denominational background means that a significant number of invitations have come from ecumenical groups. The last few years have seen Community teams sharing in a large ecumenical mission in Milton Keynes, in the contrasting areas of Westbury-on-Trym and Kingswood, Bristol, and a visit to Jersey, which saw for the first time virtually all the churches on the island working together.

Carrying out this expansion of the training and outreach ministry has necessitated some significant alterations in the Community's life. The balance of the year has changed, now that the winter period, traditionally regarded as a time to relax and take things easier, has become as busy, if not

busier, than the summer houseparty season; not an easy
adjustment for those accustomed to the former pattern of
life. It is taking time to discover the right balance between
rest and activity, so as to harness the full potential of the
Community. The new programme is also very dependent
on the quality of Community members, which since the
earliest days has been recognised as a key factor in Lee
Abbey's effectiveness. Here a trend has been the growth
both in the numbers and the maturity of those seeking to
join Community – there are far more suitable applicants
than can ever be considered. Notable also is that the
majority of the younger, short-term Community members
now offer to stay for at least two years, thus providing
greater continuity in the work. This reflects a general
movement throughout the Church with more young people
seeking opportunities for Christian service.

Expansion of the work has not meant any marked increase in the overall number of the Community members.
What is different is that the Community is now maintained
at full strength throughout the year, while before there had
always been a decline in numbers at the end of the
houseparty season. Streamlining of administration and
re-equipment have helped to increase the efficiency of
departmental work and so make the best use of Community
members.

The one significant increase in manpower has been in the
pastoral team, with two additional Chaplains; one with
special responsibility for co-ordinating the outreach programme, and the other for overseeing the student work and
developing links with colleges and schools. Two further
additions have been a member of the Community with
full-time responsibility for music, dance and drama, and
another to develop the use of audio-visual resources, running a tape service and co-ordinating the use of films, video
and other visual aids. Their work is all part of the policy for
the Community to make full use of all available resources in
its ministry. It also demonstrates to guests the potential for

communicating the Gospel to be found in latent gifts in the congregation, and the use of published material.

As Community members have been encouraged to discover their own distinctive gifts, so fresh resources for ministry have emerged. This has been seen particularly in the use of music, dance, drama and testimony as a powerful means of presenting some aspect of the Christian faith.

Among all the changes one thing that has not altered has been the continued, humbling evidence of God at work in changing people's lives. With St. Paul, Lee Abbey cannot help but conclude that it 'is not ashamed of the Gospel, it is the power of God for salvation to everyone who has faith.'

As a housewife from Hampshire wrote after a house-party,

> I cannot cease to thank and praise Him for His love, forgiveness and the power of His infilling, which continued daily, driving out all negative thoughts of fear, lack of confidence, insecurity, etc., and replacing these with His love, power and assurance of His abiding presence. There really aren't sufficient words to describe this great joy within me like a force welling up and overflowing . . . several of the folk at church have noticed the difference, and it has been a great joy to be able to say Who has made the difference but most important of all my husband knows that I have been changed. He admits that he doesn't understand yet but it's wonderful to be able to openly share with him what God is doing for me.

The experience of many people is summed up by a Rural Dean from the Cotswolds, reflecting the impact that had been made on a group from his deanery,

> Lee Abbey is a living demonstration of all the promises Jesus makes. One is so conscious of His Living Presence there, and you must have been aware of the many

blessings the Holy Spirit poured out on the members of our party. Healing of hurts, tensions, physical disabilities, change and new life for a number, new vision, new sense of purpose, new love and understanding.

## Postscript

As we enter the eighties, the name of Lee Abbey is known all over the world. There are countless men and women who can testify to their lives being touched by God through its ministry, and many churches have discovered fresh direction and vision for their work. In many places there are Christian communities who trace their initial inspiration to what was pioneered in that virtually derelict hotel in remote North Devon.

By material standards it has been a great success; the house and estate are set in order, and well filled with guests in Devon and students in London.

Yet this has been a story about the work of God, not the achievements of man. It has been about faith and not success. This same daring faith is as necessary now as it was in the forties, if God is to continue to use Lee Abbey. Many challenging issues will need to be faced in faith.

A firm foundation may have been laid and the present policy may be clear, but the constant care must be to hear the Word of God, and to be obedient to the leading of the Spirit. It would be good to think that should God one day call the fellowship to shut up the property in Devon or in London and embark on some different work, then there would be the faith to obey.

The beauty of the view from the front of the house overlooking Lee Bay and the estate continues to catch the breath of all who come.

> Happy my lot cast in so fair a ground,
> Where Exmoor flings down to the Devon seas,
> Her buttress hillsides thick with wind-swept trees,
> And giant cliffs stand sentinel around.

So wrote Jack Winslow in one of his poems. Yet this view does not remain static. Many of the trees, planted by Squire Bailey in the middle of the last century, are nearing the end of their life. A massive programme of replanting is being undertaken and within a few years the hillside will have taken on a new appearance – as beautiful but different. So must be the work of Lee Abbey.

> Do not cling to the events of the past
> Or dwell on what happened long ago.
> Watch for the new thing I am going to do.
> It is happening already – you can see it now!

(Isaiah 43: 18, 19)

# Appendix

## Chairmen of the Lee Abbey Council

| | |
|---|---|
| Roger de Pemberton | 1944 |
| Cuthbert Bardsley – Bishop of Croydon | 1946 |
| Geoffrey Rogers | 1948 |
| Cuthbert Bardsley – Bishop of Croydon – Bishop of Coventry | 1950 |
| Gordon Strutt – Bishop of Stockport | 1967 |
| Denis Wakeling – Bishop of Southwell | 1977 |

## Wardens of Lee Abbey

| | |
|---|---|
| Roger de Pemberton | 1946 |
| Geoffrey Rogers | 1950 |
| Ken Pillar | 1965 |
| Geoffrey Paul | 1971 |
| John Perry | 1977 |

## Wardens of the Lee Abbey International Students Club

| | |
|---|---|
| Gordon Mayo | 1964 |
| Chris Hayward | 1971 |
| David Johnson | 1974 |
| Derek Barnes | 1977 |
| John Watson | 1981 |

A Church of England Holiday Centre

# LEE ABBEY
## LYNTON

Training
Courses

Tennis
Riding

House
Parties

Boating
Hiking

# DEVON

**Loveliest in Spring**

**Glorious in Summer and Autumn**

**Best for Winter Holidays**

## OPEN ALL THE YEAR ROUND
(Except Oct. 13—Nov. 10)

## FOR RECREATION and RENEWAL

Fees — from 4 gns. per week

Prospectus and full details from the Secretary, Lee Abbey, Lynton, N.Devon.
Tel. Lynton 2103

**or locally from**

# LEE ABBEY
## Re-union

AND

## Mass Meeting

Central Hall, Westminster, S.W.1.

# Saturday, Oct. 25th

## RE-UNION 3 p.m.

Chairman : The Rev. GEOFFREY J. ROGERS.

Speakers : A LEE ABBEY TEAM.

## MASS MEETING 6 p.m.

## "THE CHRISTIAN ADVANCE."

Chairman : The Rev. GEOFFREY J. ROGERS.

Speaker : The Rev. LESLIE WRIGHT, Chaplain in Chief, R.A.F.

## SUNDAY, OCTOBER 26TH.

| | | |
|---|---|---|
| 11.30 a.m. | St. Martin-in-the-Fields ... | The Rev. GEOFFREY J. ROGERS |
| 11 a.m. | St. Leonard's, Streatham ... | The Rev. JACK C. WINSLOW |
| 6.30 p.m. | Holy Trinity, Brompton ... | The Rev. JACK C. WINSLOW |
| | St. Marks, Kennington ... | H. LESLIE SUTTON, Esq. |
| | St. Matthews, Surbiton ... | The Rev. GEOFFREY J. ROGERS |

REEVES, PRINTER, LYNTON.

Colleen Townsend Evans

# THE VINE LIFE

Colleen Townsend Evans gets back to basics in her search for what it really means to 'abide in the Vine'. Christ's challenging words are brought into new focus as she shares her discoveries.

'This book has thrown fresh light and new insights into John 15. It gets right to the heart of the matter and holds the attention from start to finish, illuminated as it is by unforgettable illustrations' *Ruth Bell Graham, wife of Billy Graham.*

James and Marti Hefley

# UNSTILLED VOICES

Twenty-five years ago the world was stunned by the massacre of five young missionaries by the 'most hostile savages known' – the Auca Indians of Ecuador. These fearless Christians had denied themselves, leaving home and families, only to die. But that was not the end. The wife of one and the sister of another decided to carry on the mission.

*Unstilled Voices* provides an inspiring insight into the growth of the Auca church today, and considers the remarkable story of the impact that these events are having on the church of tomorrow.

# Tom Walker

# RENEW US BY YOUR SPIRIT

*Foreword by David Watson.*

Has the renewal of the Holy Spirit now had its day? 'Emphatically no!', insists Tom Walker, and reveals why in this heart-warming and perceptive book. A lively church before renewal. St John's Harborne has continued to grow. New styles of worship and new structures have been developed, never losing sight of the power of the Spirit and Christ's call to love.